BISON
BOOKS

Charley Hester, 1907

The True Life Wild West Memoir of a Bush-Popping Cow Waddy

Charley Hester

Edited by Kirby Ross

University of Nebraska Press
Lincoln

Library of Congress Cataloging-in-
Publication Data
Hester, Charley, 1853–1940.
The true life Wild West memoir of a
bush-popping cow waddy / Charley
Hester; edited by Kirby Ross.
p.   cm.
Includes bibliographical references.
ISBN 0-8032-7346-0 (pbk.: alk. paper)
1. Hester, Charley, 1853–1940.
2. Cowboys—West (U.S.)—Biography.
3. West (U.S.)—Biography. 4. Ranch
life—West (U.S.) 5. West (U.S.)—
Social life and customs—19th century.
6. Frontier and pioneer life—West
(U.S.) 7. Outlaws—West (U.S.)—Biography—Anecdotes. I. Ross, Kirby.
II. Title.
F596.H47   2004
978′.02′092—dc22
2004003156

To Charley's granddaughter
Fern Elder
1910–2002

Contents

The World of Charley Hester

Maps

Introduction

•◆ Kirby Ross

Growing up in Phillips County, Kansas, I was given to the idea that the family to which I belong had a run-of-the-mill rural history, something along the lines of British forebears migrating to the New World, where they took up a life in agriculture, after which—as my thinking went—these ancestors begat a three-hundred-year line of farmers and did nothing spectacular in the way of leaving a mark on the history of the nation. Despite this, upon occasion I would hear various stories from the old-timers of my childhood, stories that I took as being tall tales since they sometimes concerned this uncle being scalped by Indians, that uncle being killed by Jesse James, and so on.

Around five years ago I began a somewhat casual scholarly search into my roots—a search that soon expanded in scope. Driven by a strong interest in history and aided by an educational and professional background in the art of research, I was quite successful in verifying old family stories and uncovering new ones. These stories concerned patriots who fought for the creation and continued existence of our nation, pioneers who braved the trails to Oregon, 49ers who sought their fortunes in the gold fields of California, and yes, uncles who were launched into eternity by Indians and desperadoes.

One of the stories of my youth concerned "Grandpa Graybeard." His daughter—my great-grandmother, Eva Marie Hester Peugh (1885–1985)—regaled family members with her experiences as a little girl coming west with him in a covered wagon and settling on a homestead in northeastern Phillips County on the state line just south of Naponee, Nebraska. While her mild-mannered stories about living in a sod house and becoming a teacher at age sixteen were somewhat fresh coming in first-person form, more mysterious and vague were the secondhand stories of her father's early life—the adventurous life he led before he became a dirt farmer and family man on the dusty, arid croplands of the Kansas High Plains.

Old Charley Hester, so it was told, had once been a cowboy on the Chisholm Trail. He ran away from home in his mid-teens, headed for Texas, and in the process met Wild Bill Hickok, chased buffalo, and tangled with Indians. One version that made the rounds in my extended family held that Charley was even the pattern for Errol Flynn's character in the 1939 movie Dodge City. So it was told.

Then several years ago my grandmother, Fern Elder, gave me a box of Hester memorabilia in recognition of my role as family historian. This box contained a variety of photographs and documents, including a 1939 newspaper clipping reporting how Warner Brothers interviewed Charley at his home three times during the making of Dodge City. Considering this, while I hardly think he was the inspiration for the Errol Flynn character, it does seem he was a consultant for the overall story.

One other item given to me by my grandmother was of a sort very important to any family research. In fact, it was the Holy Grail of my family research, a document whose significance I immediately recognized. This dramatic item was old Grandpa Graybeard's story as it was recorded by an acquaintance, E. S. Sutton. More specifically and importantly, it was the personal memoir of his life riding the Texas trails in the 1870s.

As I looked further into this chapter of family history, my research took me to Dundy County, Nebraska, where the name "Hester" is gold—in part because of Charley but also because of other members of his immediate family. The museum in Benkelman, the county seat, maintains a Hester Room, and the Sarah Ann Hester Memorial Home, named for Charley's mother (my own great-great-great grandmother), sits on a hill that overlooks the town.

In the course of several trips to the area, I discovered bits and pieces of interesting trivia, including, for example, the fact that a Hester barn photo once appeared in the World Book Encyclopedia entry for Nebraska, and that there is a Hester Road in the southern part of the county. I also found that E. S. Sutton was an amateur but avid Dundy County historian who had been born in Naponee, where Charley had known Sutton's parents in the 1890s (see "Charley's Acquaintance with E. S. Sutton"). Apparently, over the first decades of the twentieth century, Sutton personally recorded the early life's journey of his old family friend, Charley.

The True Life Wild West Memoir of a Bush-Popping Cow Waddy is the story of that journey, told in Charley's own words. Most of it comes from the document given to me by my grandmother, with two minor exceptions. Those exceptions concern the newspaper article in the prologue as well as additions to stories about Scorpion Pete found in chapters 26 and 29. The newspaper article in the prologue is presented merely to set up the narrative. As for the Scorpion Pete anecdotes, a slightly different account that provides additional detail was used in a 1968 Sutton anthology entitled *Teepees to Soddies*. For the purposes of the Hester book I have integrated parts of that version into the original memoir.

A brief note on the spelling of Charley's name: The newspaper article spelled it "Charlie;" the memoir, "Charley." I have kept both as originally presented. Assuming a personal memoir to have a more accurate spelling than a newspaper article, I defer to the second spelling in my own use of the name.

I have endeavored to keep my imprint on the memoir to a minimum. My annotations—the notes to the memoir chapters and the text and notes of "The World of Charley Hester"—were included to add context to matters mentioned in the primary text. Furthermore, the original memoir had no chapters, did not run chronologically, and scattered multiple references to single events somewhat haphazardly throughout. It also used commas to the extreme, had sentences dozens of words in length, and paragraphs that ran ad infinitum. I have tried to limit my editing to enhancing the flow of the story while leaving the original flavor and tone intact (e.g., combining scattered references to single events into single chapters and cropping exceedingly long sentences and paragraphs into multiple ones). As for flavor, the cowboy verses found in my edited version are from the original (presumably as recalled by Charley) as are the misspellings and phrasing. The chapter arrangement is mine, and—but for the occasional subheading from the original—the chapter headings are also mine. Finally, my numbered notes found in the memoir generally provide brief additional information on matters referred to by Charley. However, when my research revealed information too lengthy to be covered in a brief note, I compiled those additional details into full chapters at the back of this book in the section called "The World of Charley Hester." To advise the reader to consult this information, I have inserted the names of the chapters in brackets in the memoir text.

Charley's Childhood

To provide a further framework to Charley's memoir, I also uncovered the story of the life that he led before and after his days working as a cowhand in the 1870s, as well as the broader, compelling story of the Hester family. By the time Charley set out on the Chisholm Trail, his family had been established in America for over 170 years. A great-grandson of a veteran of the Revolutionary War, Charley was also the oldest child of David Hester and his second wife, Sarah Ann Hallam. Born in Pattonsburg, Illinois, on January 30, 1853, Charley was raised near Cornell and had five older half-brothers and sisters through his father's deceased first wife, Jane McKinney Hester.[1]

One early memory Charley had from his childhood was watching two of those half-brothers march off to war to fight for the Union. Neither would return home. Back in Livingston County the family continued to expand—including Charley, seven children had been born to Sarah Ann by 1865. Then, in November of that year, with Sarah pregnant for the eighth time in a little over a dozen years, David caught typhoid fever and died. Ten weeks later, widowed Sarah gave birth to twins.[2]

With the Hesters having one of the larger farming operations in the county, holding hearth and home together was a responsibility that Sarah took on with determination. In speaking of her "no give attitude," a great-granddaughter noted that "on her fell the burden of survival for her sons and daughters and her life became one of hard work and perseverance. Her children's early memories of her were of her always working to feed and clothe them. They said she could shoot and butcher a cow or hog as well as any man. She was a large and strong woman which probably served her well for what her life was to become."[3]

Sarah also relied heavily on a strong religious background (several of her brothers were ministers) as well as an equally strong personal will and discipline. According to a granddaughter, "she suffered many hardships bravely for she was left a widow with a large family to care for and no funds except that which she could earn with her hands by weaving and adding the earnings from the Illinois farm. No luxuries were to be found in this humble home. No cakes or sugar were to be had. Just the bare necessities to sustain life."[4]

Farmer

It was in this atmosphere that a teenage Charley Hester "felt the urge of making his own way, so he left the little home and went to Missouri and on through to Texas," where he undertook the adventure of a lifetime. After the cattle drive of 1878 profiled in this book, Charley returned home to Cornell and married Hattie King four years later. Following the wedding the newlyweds left for Marshall County, Iowa, where four children were born to the couple over the next decade.[5]

In 1892 Charley loaded his family and possessions into a covered wagon and moved further west to settle on land in Sumner Township, Phillips County, Kansas, not far from the homes of his brothers John and Elmer, who had preceded him to the region. There Charley had three more children, including a boy who died five days before his first birthday. After Charley had spent two decades in Phillips County, his "fat and itchy feet" took him onward, and in February of 1913, with almost one-third of his life yet ahead of him, he moved to Dundy County, Nebraska. Upon his arrival he joined a family enterprise begun by his aging mother that was expanding to unimagined proportions.[6]

"God Gave My Brother Elmer the Brains"

Like his older brother Charley, Elmer Hester started out as a bit of a wanderer, trying to find his place in life. In the early 1880s he moved with his mother and brother John to Oxford, Nebraska, and shortly after returned to Illinois to attend the Dixon Business College while John took up farming near Naponee. Sarah, now in her sixties, migrated on to Dundy County, and by using the homestead laws as well as funds obtained from the sale of the Illinois farm (Charley quit-claimed his share over), began acquiring the property that laid the foundation to a ranching empire.[7]

After finishing school, Elmer and his twin brother, Eli, moved to Colorado and established claims on farmland near Arikaree, in southeast Washington County. Eli ultimately forfeited the rights to his property and joined his mother in Dundy County, while Elmer carried on alone in the midst of what he later described as the most trying time of his life. After perfecting his ownership to the land in 1890 he went briefly to Dundy County to teach during the 1890–91 school term, and then on to Phillips County, where he taught at the Lone Tree School from 1891 to 1895.[8] Finally, Elmer returned to Dundy County and put down roots that lasted the remainder of his life. Shortly after he made this final move, most of the rest of the Hester clan who were not already there soon followed and also procured land in the area.[9]

Over the following years, Elmer and Eli separately consolidated the family web of Dundy County holdings under their own control and further expanded by taking advantage of various government programs, such as the Kincaid Act and Tree Claims Act. After selling his Arikaree property and obtaining a personal loan from Charley, Elmer was able to finance the purchase of a herd of cattle, thus giving birth to the Wineglass Ranch a dozen miles north of Parks, Nebraska. Upon reaching this point, it was said of the Hesters, "It seemed they moved mountains."[10]

Rancher

In 1913, seeking new challenges, Charley took on the oversight of the

Hester Riverside Ranch interests a couple of miles southwest of Parks. Within months Hattie passed away and Charley took her to Naponee to lay her to rest next to their infant son. Then a second blow struck the family the following year as the tough matriarch, Sarah Ann Hester, died at age ninety-one.[11]

Throughout the early twentieth century, Elmer directed an expansion that resulted in the acquisition of the Cottonwood Ranch, the Memorial Ranch, and the Evans Ranch locally, in addition to Kansas wheatland as far south as Kanorado. Elmer and Charley concentrated on raising registered purebred Nebraska Herefords—a long evolution from the cantankerous Texas longhorns with which Charley had begun. Their efforts to develop a superior bloodline advanced when they made the high bid for a top Hereford bull at the 1936 National Western Stock Show in Denver. From this purchase the prize-winning Prince Dundy line was developed.[12]

As the years passed Charley continued working the range until finally, in the late 1930s, his earlier life caught up to him. At that time E. S. Sutton took an interest in his stories of Wild Bill Hickok and Wyatt Earp and life on the Chisholm and Western cattle trails. The press joined in, and before long Charley's celebrity began to grow; it reached its peak after researchers from Warner Brothers visited with the aged cowpoke several times during the making of *Dodge City*.

Not long after the movie's release, the end of the trail came for Old Charley. With his passing on August 12, 1940, the drifting cow waddy had one final journey yet to make—back to Naponee to join Hattie after a quarter century's separation.

Hester Legacy

Elmer's star continued to burn bright. In the course of his life in Dundy County, he served as president of the Farmers and Merchants Bank, president of the Dundy County Stock Growers Association, and chairman of the Methodist Church board of trustees. In 1944 he established a charitable trust as a precursor to the creation of the Sarah Ann Hester Memorial Home. With his donation of four thousand acres of his land holdings to the project, a permanent economic base to support the institution was secured.[13]

Upon his death five years later, the full extent of Uncle Elmer's gifts became fully realized, for which the *History of Dundy County* praised him as being "probably Dundy County's greatest philanthropist." Hester ministerial scholarships were established at the Iliff School of Theology in Denver and Nebraska Wesleyan University in Lincoln. Both institutions received additional donations to benefit their construction programs. Bequests were also made to the Benkelman Methodist Church and the Benkelman Cemetery. Finally, the Elmer E. Hester Foundation was created and endowed with his beloved Wineglass Ranch along with four hundred head of Hereford cattle, bringing the sum total of his 1940s gifts to over 8,400 acres. The Hester Foundation exists to provide for religious and vocational education as well as 4-H Club work, Boy and Girl Scouts, and other similar youth activities.[14]

In recognition of their pioneer spirit and local prominence, as well as the good works left in their wake, a room to the entire Hester family has been dedicated at the Dundy County Historical Society-Museum in Benkelman. Showcasing photographs, documents, personal possessions, and other items, the museum has succeeded in establishing a noteworthy tribute to the Hester legacy.

Cracker or Cake

A reader especially well-versed in the Old West will see a few discrepancies between Charley's description of people and events in his memoir and that which is commonly believed or recorded elsewhere. For example, a question exists as to whether Joel Collins rode the cow trail with Charley before Collins outlawed with Sam Bass. One of the purposes behind my annotations is to note and provide insights into these differences, as well as to present possible explanations for them.

E. S. Sutton once offered a thoughtful observation about differing personal accounts of the West—a perspective more ably told in just a few words than I can provide in many. In the foreword to *Teepees to Soddies*, speaking specifically of the anecdotes of Charley Hester and other authentic Old West cowboys he met, Sutton noted: "We recognize this will dispute some currently accepted stories which were handed down from one to another in good faith, but often became mixed in the batter and ended a cracker instead of a cake."

Whether it be cracker or cake, what follows is the story of Charley Hester.

⚘ Notes ⚘

Introduction

1. "Obituary, Charles Albert Hester," *Franklin County* (NE) *Sentinel*, August 22, 1940; Irene Hester Lawrence, "Charles Albert Hester," October 15, 1989 (typescript in possession of Kirby Ross); Delphia Hester Burr, "Hester, Sarah Ann (Hallam)," *History of Dundy County, Nebraska 1880–1987* (Dallas TX: Curtis Media, 1988), 454. See also Hester Geraldine Lester Searl, *Hester Genealogy: A Story of Some Descendants of John Hester* (Patterson CA: n.p., 1972). Irene Lawrence was the daughter of Charley Hester, and Delphia Burr is the granddaughter of Charley's brother Eli. Hester Searl was a distant relative who compiled a comprehensive genealogical history of the various branches of the Hester family.

2. "Obituary, Charles Albert Hester"; Lawrence, "Charles Albert Hester"; Burr, "Hester, Sarah Ann (Hallam)," 454; Delphia Hester Burr, "Hester, Elmer Elsworth and Minnie (Kimberling)," *History of Dundy County, Nebraska 1880–1987* (1988), 453–54; Adah Hester Young, "Sarah Ann Hester," *Sarah Ann Hester Memorial Home for the Aging: A Nebraska Methodist Conference Institution* (Benkelman NE, 1968), 3. Adah Young was the daughter of Charley's brother John.

3. Burr, "Hester, Sarah Ann (Hallam)," 454. Valued at almost $5,000, the farm was worth significantly more than most others in the area. See U.S. Bureau of the Census, *Ninth U.S. Census for Amity Township, Livingston County, Illinois* (1870).

4. Young, "Sarah Ann Hester," 3.

5. "Obituary, Charles Albert Hester"; Lawrence, "Charles Albert Hester."

6. "Obituary, Charles Albert Hester"; Lawrence, "Charles Albert Hester"; Hester family lore: Fern Elder, Arletta Roundtree, Phyllis Hutchinson, Lois

Broyles, Everett Smith. Fern Elder was the granddaughter of Charley Hester; Arletta Roundtree, the wife of one of his grandsons; and the others, his great-grandchildren.

7. John Faris, ed., *Who's Who in Nebraska* (Lincoln: Nebraska Press Association, 1940), 409; E. S. Sutton, *Teepees to Soddies* (1968), 108; Burr, "Hester, Sarah Ann (Hallam)," 453–54.

8. Faris, ed., *Who's Who in Nebraska*, 409; Sutton, *Teepees to Soddies*, 108; Burr, "Hester, Sarah Ann (Hallam)," 453–54; Delphia Hester Burr, "Hester, Eli and Carrie (Strobridge)," *History of Dundy County, Nebraska 1880–1987* (1988), 452–53; Elmer E. Hester Land Patent, Book 144, 1–4 S., R.50–R.51W, 6S, p. 157, Sterling Land Office, Records of the Bureau of Land Management, Record Group 49, National Archives and Records Administration—Rocky Mountain Region (Denver).

9. Burr, "Hester, Elmer Elsworth," 453; Hester family lore.

10. Burr, "Hester, Elmer Elsworth," 453; Hester family lore; Sutton, *Teepees to Soddies*, 108; Delphia Hester Burr, "Hester," *Dundy County Heritage* (1976), 138.

11. Lawrence, "Charles Albert Hester"; Hester family lore. Although the Riverside Ranch is no longer in the family, to this day a major north-south secondary road into Kansas that abuts the ranch is called Hester Road. See *Nebraska Atlas & Gazetteer* (Yarmouth ME: DeLorme, 2000), 68.

12. Lawrence, "Charles Albert Hester"; Hester family lore; Sutton, *Teepees to Soddies*, 108; Burr, "Elmer Elsworth Hester," 453. Apparently reflecting the family's earlier wanderlust, Elmer named another one of his most valuable bulls Vagabond Dundy. See *In the Matter of the Estate of Elmer E. Hester*, Case No. 1033 (Cty. Ct. Dundy County NE 1949).

13. Faris, *Who's Who in Nebraska*, 409; Sutton, *Teepees to Soddies*, 108; Burr, "Hester," 140; Burr, "Elmer Elsworth Hester" and "Hester, Sarah Ann (Hallam)," 453, 454; "Sarah Ann Hester Memorial Home," *History of Dundy County, Nebraska 1880–1987* (1988), 128–29; "History of Sarah Ann Hester Memorial Home" (typescript produced by the Sarah Ann Hester Memorial Home). Despite his philanthropy, Elmer has a reputation both locally and within the family as having been a somewhat ruthless businessman.

14. Faris, *Who's Who in Nebraska*, 409; Sutton, *Teepees to Soddies*, 108; Burr, "Hester," 140; Burr, "Elmer Elsworth Hester" and "Hester, Sarah Ann (Hallam)," 453, 454; "Sarah Ann Hester Memorial Home," *History of Dundy County, Nebraska*, 128–29; "History of Sarah Ann Hester Memorial Home"; Wade

Stevens, "Elmer E. Hester," *Sarah Ann Hester Memorial Home for the Aging: A Nebraska Methodist Conference Institution* (Benkelman NE, 1968), 5; Articles of Incorporation of the Elmer E. Hester Foundation, State of Nebraska Department of State, December 29, 1947; Articles of Amendment to the Articles of Incorporation of the Elmer E. Hester Foundation, State of Nebraska Secretary of State, March 27, 1989; *Dundy County Public School District v. Lincoln Foundation, Inc.*, Case No. 4563 (Dist. Ct. Dundy County NE 1987).

"God gave my brother the brains
and me the fat and itchy feet."

❧ Charles Albert Hester
1853–1940

The True
Life Wild
West Memoir
of a Bush-
Popping
Cow Waddy

Part One

*Over the
Chisholm
Trail, 1871*

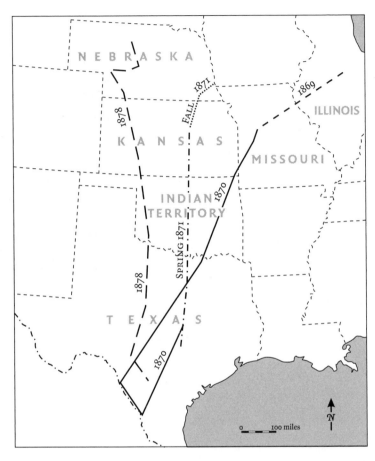

Map of Trails Traveled

Prologue

Warner Brothers Studio

Charlie Hester Knew Dodge City History

If and when Charlie Hester goes to see the great movie production "Dodge City" which depicts the West in the making, he will be in a different position than most of us because he will be checking it for authenticity while the younger generation will be looking back into an age of which they know but little except through the medium of reading and through conversation with folks like Charlie.

Long before anyone hereabouts knew that there would be such a production as "Dodge City," Charlie was being contacted by bibliographers for the Warner Brothers Company who were then preparing to produce the great western movie.

Three times they sent research men to Benkelman to interview Mr. Hester as to certain details and conditions during the early days at Dodge City and to ask him to check on certain phases of the story being incorporated in the production. And Charlie didn't disappoint them because he knows his stuff when it comes to pioneering days in the West, and as you watch the great drama as it unfolds at the Zorn Theater on the first four nights of next week, you will possibly see some features that Charlie had a hand in recalling from memory.

Mr. Hester, who is now past 86 years of age, spent most of his life on the western frontier and he lived where the pioneering spirit was at its crest in such spots as the famous Dodge City, railroad outpost, cattle center and goal of thousands of fortune hunters, gamblers, home-seekers, cowboys and what have you.

Mr. Hester is still in reasonably good health and is at present visiting with his daughter at Denver. Since "Dodge City" is being brought to Denver for its first appearance in that city this week, it is possible that Charlie might get to see it a few days ahead of Benkelman folks, but not too many days before.

→ Benkelman Post, April 21, 1939

Chapter One
Restless Spirit, 1869

The post–Civil War depression settled heavily over our part of Illinois. There was very little for a young man to do and there was no opportunity for him to purchase land, it being too high in price, too low in value to pay out. Soldiers returning from the war tried to settle down, but their restless spirit urged them to seek homes on the Frontier. Occasionally a man returned from a trip to Kansas or Texas with tall tales about hunting buffalo, Indian fights and trailing cattle. The newspapers carried many interesting accounts of adventure, of new farmland to be had for the taking, and of great opportunities awaiting the man with the determination to win. All of this fired my imagination and as the sun set each evening I would stand entranced in day dreams, visioning myself out there in the land of romance and adventure. Several of my friends discussed a trip with me, and at last fourteen of us decided to see what the West had to offer. So with dreams of adventure, at the age of sixteen I cut loose from home ties and with my friends we left Livingston County, Illinois, for Missouri.

We traveled on horseback and soon overtook a convoy of wagons and decided to throw in with them for safety's sake. Bushwhackers and bandits infested the sparsely settled country and no person's property was safe from their raiding bands unless well protected. More than one traveler was robbed of money and horse and considered themselves lucky if they escaped with their lives. We did not intend to be caught unawares.

We arrived in western Missouri in December 1869, and stayed in that section of the country for a spell before going on into Texas. While I did not know it at the time, in Missouri we were in the country of the notorious bank robbers and bandits, the James boys and the Youngers. It seems one must get away from a country to hear the latest gossip and get the juiciest tales concerning its badmen.

At one time we had some of our horses stray from the pasture and my three-year-old mare started back home to Illinois. She was found at Chalk Cliff where I went to prove her. On my way down I passed the caves on the Osage where the James boys sometimes "holed up" after committing a robbery. It was a rugged beautiful country and many times in my later years fighting hot winds, dust, and grasshoppers in Phillips County, Kansas, I wished I was back in western Missouri fishing along those shady, cool creeks.

Early in March we again took the trail to the southwest. This time there were fifteen of us in the cavalcade, all with horses. Others had fallen in who had wagons of various sorts, so it made quite a party. In reality there were two separate parties, the one I was with being headed by a Mr. Golden, while the other group was headed by Mr. Woods.[1] However, we camped together.

There were two fiddles in the outfit, and two dern good fiddlers. How they could hoe down the row. Usually we were pretty tired by nightfall, but never too tired to enjoy the music. When we arrived at a settlement, the boys would put on a dance. Girls were scarce at these places, but old and young turned out and we always had a fine time. Several times we put on a stag dance, and to make the dance more interesting some of the boys draped their coats around their waists to simulate skirts. They acted the part of "ladies" to perfection, and it was really amusing to see how serious and gentlemanly the rough-shod men carried them.

Chapter Two
Snipe Hunting

In our outfit was a man named Booth. He was an ignorant sort of a hillbilly and was the butt of all sorts of jokes. You can believe me when I say there was plenty of jokes—a gang of fifteen lads do not overlook a single bet. I, being the youngest of the gang, was the one Booth usually tried to even scores on—and he took me for more than one merry chase.

One evening he secretly organized a snipe hunt and I was invited. At first I thought the gang was after Booth, but soon it dawned on me that I was to be the victim and I decided to play along with them.

At that time we stayed at a little place in Henry County named Clinton. Two of the Clinton men were to be ring leaders. One of them had just purchased a new lantern, which was handed to me along with a sack and a couple of sticks which were to be used to keep the sack open. They placed me on Cabin Creek, some three miles from camp, and instructed me to wait there very quietly with the lighted lantern and open sack, while they took Booth up the creek where he would start driving the snipes down to me.

It was one of those intensely dark nights. The atmosphere was sticky and oppressive which indicated a storm was brewing. I was located under a huge sycamore tree, which would be some protection in case of a storm, but I did not intend to wait.

Assuming I was ignorant of the procedure of a snipe hunt, these men would have given it away for as soon as they thought they were out of hearing they began to laugh and joke about it, and the still night air carried their voices. After they had got well up the creek they began to call back to say they were running in the snipes, warning me to be very quiet, and admonishing me to stay right there as it would be quite awhile before the wary birds would come to the light.

I did not wait any longer. I threw the lantern and sack in the creek and struck out for camp. Almost immediately I ran into something that put my hair on end and lightning in my feet. As I stumbled over the object, it came to life with a woof-woof, and down I went, right into a litter of pigs. They were as scared as I but they didn't travel half as fast. I got to camp all right and snooked into bed without anyone seeing me. Then it began to rain and how it did rain.

Sometime later I heard the boys sloushing into camp, complaining of the soaking they got. Mr. Golden said to Tom Huston: "I am worried about Hester. He was left out on Cabin Creek and it will raise quickly and the damn fool is apt to drown." Tom then became concerned and before long the bunch pulled out for the creek. Of course they didn't find me and it was a mighty worried bunch that returned to camp two hours later. They had found no evidence of me and they were all discussing my fate as they shivered in the dark. I heard one of the men say in much disgust, "Damn him, if he wants to drown, let him drown!" Shortly after, my partner came to the wagon and crawled into bed and when he found me there you could have heard his yell to Kingdom Come.

It was a sickly, sheepish looking bunch of men I faced, and the one who had done the cussing acted like a mutt who had got caught kissing the servant girl. Golden asked me what I did. I told him I fixed the sack as instructed and in a few minutes so many snipes came rushing into the sack that they wobbled into the creek. In doing so they knocked the lantern into the creek also. I then hurried home as it looked like rain. That sure got their goats. They never again inquired about the lantern or sack. They knew what really happened. Next day Booth went to town and bought a new lantern. It took a lot of "white mule" to knock the chills they contracted and to cheer them up.

Chapter Three

Southdown Country

In due course we went southwest through Baxter Springs, Kansas, to Fort Gibson in the Indian Territory. As we traveled we followed very close to the present Missouri-Kansas-Texas Railroad.[1] Every stream had either a toll-bridge or a ferry-boat charter. There was no avoiding this highway robbery either—it was a case of taking it and liking it although there was plenty of cussing.

An old Indian had a steam ferry across the Gibson River at Fort Gibson.[2] The Arkansas River at this point is a sandy, dirty, boiling stream, while the Gibson runs clear and clean. It was really a marvelous and a worthwhile sight to observe how far the current ran out into the Arkansas before being absorbed by the muddier stream.

We had two long drives to make without water. One was a thirty-mile stretch as we went out of Missouri into Kansas and the other was in the I.T. An Indian woman had a well there, which was the only watering place, and we had to make that well at noon. The day before we arrived some 125 wagons stopped at her place for water. She made good money at the game and no one could avoid paying her tribute to her. This place was called Boggy Depot.

We followed the road and crossed the Red River above Sherman, Texas. There was nothing but open prairie where Denison now stands. Soon we cut loose from the wagoneers who spread out over the country headed for various places and for various purposes. Our outfit continued to Eagle Pass and thence down the Rio Grand river and back to the "Southdown" country in Bell county [see "Southdown Country"]. There we found the area literally overrun with cattle. About all they were worth was their hide and tallow, and the ticks saw to it that there was precious little tallow.

Overgrazing the range contributed its share of woes to the ranchers who had been unable to find markets for their surplus stock, except to trail them north, which at that time was uncertain and expensive in both labor and loss of stock. Indian depredations contributed an extra thorn or two for the stockmen. So it was a case of moving the cattle north or keeping them.

I hired on with an outfit where the Boss went in with a neighbor and in a manner they put their ranches together as they had about the same number of acres and cattle. At first they tried using men from both outfits but this always led to trouble, so they hit on the idea of dividing the time.

None of the range was fenced. Generally the cattle roamed at will. However, there was a system of patrolling the range which kept the cattle from drifting too far. Riders were stationed on the outer edge of the range and rode the line to shoo back the drifters. Our range line was approximately twenty-five miles long and men were stationed at both ends. Each day they rode until they met and then returned to camp for the night. As a rule, soddy houses or cut-banks were provided for the pokes to live in while on the line, but I have seen a wagon with a cover provided for the purpose.

Cows were generally through calving by the time grass was ready and as we worked the herd on the Southdown we made it a practice to keep the calves castrated and branded. Two of us worked a calf. The law in 1871 was that any critter without a brand after reaching the yearling age was the property of any person who slapped on an iron. Consequently everything was branded early. One might say if they were not branded as calves they never received the true owner's brand. Some one else did the branding and the brand was then respected as ownership.

The Mexican riders I ranged with were good at roping and as I was new to the game I was happy to get out of their way when they went to work. Before long I would see a piece of riding that made me "sit up and take notice." Part of the western Southdown country is thickly covered with mesquite and a scrub oak, which makes tossin' a rope a real job. However, a good cowpoke can snare a cow in tight quarters. But that was not spectacular enough for the Mexican riders. They loved to show off—and to tell the truth, you have got to hand it to those bush-poppers for being real horsemen.

They'd ride into the timber, pick their steer and then rush him. When overtaken, the rider would grab the steer's tail, give it a hitch around the saddlehorn, and then apply the spurs to his own horse. As the horse jumped forward, over went the steer. Before he could get up, the horse stopped and the rider was immediately on top of the steer. He carried short pieces of flexible rawhide rope in his belt. One of these was quickly wrapped around the critter's feet and there he was hog-tied tighter than tamrack. The horses used were especially trained for roping and a well broke horse commanded a lot of money.

Chapter Four

The Longhorns

The Southdown is a beautiful country. It lays close to the Texas mountains where numerous large springs fathered the creeks and rivers. It was the answer to the hunter's and fisherman's prayers.

Here too was the habitat of those genuine old hellions, the "Southdown Longhorns." They were usually a dun color, slab-sided as a sunfish, rangy as a starved wolf, with a big serrated backbone which connected a head at one end and a tail at the other, with four long legs spaced at each corner. It took the tail to balance the thin head which carried a pair of saber-sharp horns, God knows how wide. A perfect specimen is supposed to have a spread of horns equal to the critter's overall length. Nothing was said about how wide. I think this was the specifications laid down by Noah when he arked the critters.

Six to eight hundred pounds was their usual weight. However, those animals had a power plant like a scared coyote and it took a mighty good horse to keep up with them. They have been known to travel forty miles in a night when stampeded or when attempting to return home, and seemingly be as fresh as a daisy when morning came.

Their origin, according to authorities, was the Andalusian Longhorn. A small number were brought to Old Mexico with Cortez in 1519, along with some small Spanish horses. Within the following two hundred years the Mexicans migrated into what is now our Southwest and brought some of these tough animals with them. They took to the chaparral like flies to a sore and it was but a short time until there were many herds of the wild cattle and horses.

Both the wild variety and the more domestic ones ranged the country. Inasmuch as the hides and tallow were the only marketable parts, no attempt was made to improve the strain. When money was needed to purchase the Senora a new lace mantilla or to pay taxes the menfolk rounded up the required number of longhorns and skinned them, selling both hides and tallow.

In order to maintain the characteristic of all around cussedness, they were carriers of the Spanish fever and upon first contact with northern cattle infected them, which caused a very high mortality. At one time in the '60s practically all the domestic beef of the middle west were wiped out by this dread disease.

However, the longhorns had several points in their favor. They were prolific; they were immune to ticks and the Spanish fever; they could protect their young against prowlers; and when moved to the northern range they quickly responded to the nutritious grass of that region and made very good beef.

Some of the younger ones on the southern range did accumulate enough meat on their bones to make half way decent eating. One wit said most of the meat grew inside the horn. Another told us the best way to prepare the beef for eating was to put the horns, tail, legs, and guts (guts for seasoning) into a pot to cook. After boiling a week, scrape off the meat and then eat the horns and bones.

It was nothing unusual to see a ten-year-old critter. How do I know it was that old? Well, they claim a Southdowner will grow six inches of horn a year, just as a rattlesnake is supposed to add a button each year. If you don't believe it, just snook up on a steer, tell him to open his mouth and say a-a-a-a-h; look at his teeth, and then measure his horns. Of course that is another Texas joke. But yet the animals did reach the age of ten and even more.

Prior to 1865 there was no practical way to market them, so they ran wild. When markets did become available the longhorns played a very definite part in the economy of the Southwest. In fact they *were* the Southwest. After fulfilling their part of the program they had to move on, just as livery barns had to give way to garages.

Chapter Five

Coin of the Realm

When I was there Texas was a gold and silver state and the stores would not take Federal greenbacks. It seems the people had had a very costly experience with the Confederate shin-plasters and would take no chances with the Yankee version. It had to be "hard money" or nothing. The bankers capitalized on this and they spread the news that paper money was dangerous, but at the same time they made a good profit by charging a fee of fifteen cents or more for each greenback they exchanged for gold or silver.

There was three kinds of silver coin in circulation. It was very confusing, not to mention expensive. There was the Old Mexican silver piece, or Peso; then there was the Traders silver dollar, which I believe was minted locally; and there was the good old U.S. silver dollar. All three of them had approximately the same amounts of silver, but when the price of silver bullion dropped, the United States minted dollar held steady in value while the Traders dollar finally dropped to about forty cents. The Mexican dollar was worth more, about seventy cents, I believe.

The U.S. stamp on the minted coin was what made it worth face value. The Traders dollar was worth exactly the silver it carried. The Peso carried the same weight in silver, but it could be worked off in Mexico at face value, so it commanded a higher price locally. It was quite a game to avoid having the low value money given to you, and it was as much of a game to pass on the pieces one had accumulated.

Chapter Six
The Chisholm Trail

Down near Austin nine of us secured a job of trailing some 250 steers up the Chisholm Trail to the Nebraska City flats for a man by the name of Wier or Ware.[1] There was Joel Collins along with seven other pokes and myself. There's a place in the Indian Territory named after the Collins boys' father. Later Joel decided trail life was too hard a way to make a living. He won dubious fame as a card sharp, rustler, and train robber, but most of all for riding with the outlaw Sam Bass. I will tell about that affair later.

The original Chisholm Trail was less than two hundred miles long. Jesse Chisholm laid it out in 1865 to connect his trading post on Chisholm Creek (Wichita) with another post in the I.T. at Anadarko. Jesse had several of these stations which supplied the reservation Indians with issue goods, and he catered to the needs of the military garrisons. The odd thing about this man and the trail is that he never rode a horse on the trail, he never moved a critter over it except his ox-teams, and he was not a cattleman, but a trader.

With the first gun of the Civil War the Federal garrisons in the Southwest had found it necessary to leave immediately or else be captured by the superior Southern forces. The commanders began one of the most strategic retreats of the war. As they traveled north, other commands converged with them until they had a sizeable army. They broke new trails in places, followed old traders' trails, and they used old buffalo trails as well. They reached Fort Leavenworth in due time without the loss of a single man, beast, or wagon. It was more notable for the fact they traversed a hostile Indian country, and much of the way they broke their own trail.

It was along the Old Military Trail that Chisholm set up his trade route in '65 and two years later the Texas cattlemen followed suit. As the new cattle trail reached deeper and deeper into the South and spanned farther into the North it soon took on the name of the "Chisholm Trail" its entire length of eight hundred or nine hundred miles.

There was another man with a similar sounding name, but spelled

Chisum. John Chisum was a cattle baron, but he never traveled a mile on the Chisholm Trail. John Chisum went west into New Mexico where his huge holdings covered something over five counties, with Roswell as his headquarters. Later he made several drives with cattle to California. It was in Chisum's neck of the woods that the Lincoln County War raged for three years with the loss of twenty-five white men and no one knows how many Mexicans. Billy the Kid emerged as both the hero and villain, depending on who told the story.

Anyway, at that time there was but a few dozen miles of railroad in Texas and the nearest shipping point was on the Kansas Pacific up at Abilene, Kansas. However, another railroad was under construction (I believe it was the M.K.T.). I do recall when we later returned north up the Big Trail we crossed the newly built-up grade. I saw in the distance a two-story depot which appeared to be occupied and a well digging outfit was at work.

Once the cattle reached the rails up north on the Chisholm Trail they were in no condition to ship to the markets at Kansas City and Chicago without first having been ranged a summer on the prairies of the Indian Territory and Kansas. Some of the large Texas outfits had summer range, but most of the cattle moving in 1871 were steers that went to the feeders or they were put on grass until fat enough for market. A few herds were trailed further north into Nebraska, although I do not think many cattle reached the western part of the state at that time.[2]

There are several reasons why the Chisholm or "Big" Trail became the most famous trail in history. At the Texas end were overburdened pastures and millions of cheap cattle while at the northern end was the world's richest grasslands, connecting railroads, and the corn-belt farms which ultimately took the majority of the cattle.

The trail was hard packed and about a half mile wide, but later it spread out from one to three miles wide and was as barren as a floor in places, with the occasional narrow strips and passes where all the cattle going over the trail had to travel the exact paths.

It was held to well defined limits because of water, grass, river crossings, and some natural barriers. Indians and buffalo to the west were also deciding factors. From the south line of the Cherokee Outlet to the crossing of the Cimarron, the trail passed through the only natural opening in a black pine forest that extended many miles on either side and then ended in natural barriers of rock and creeks.[3]

Thinking about all this brings to mind an old cowboy song we would sing [see "Cowboy Songs and Verses"] on the trail—

> *I woke up one morning on the old*
>   *Chisholm Trail,*
> *Ropes in my hand and a cow*
>   *by the tail,*
> *Feet in the stirrups and*
>   *seat in the saddle,*
>   *Hi-ooo Hi-oo Yipeeee*
> *I hung and rattled with them damn*
>   *Longhorn cattle*
>   *Hi-oo Hi-ooo Yip-eeee*

As previously stated, we hit the Chisholm Trail by Austin and hied northward. I thought I was pretty well seasoned by then and tough enough to stand most any sort of saddle strain, but I soon discovered I had plenty of soft spots which turned to sore spots.[4]

The usual method of trailing was to drift the cattle until they reached water, after which they rested. Late afternoon found them drifting again and by night they would find their own bedding grounds. About all the herding done was to keep the cattle pointed in the right direction and let them take their own sweet time about it. It was foolhardy to drive the cattle while full of water. To do so caused shrinkage in weight, water sickness, and possible death. The first herds on the trail experienced heavy losses before they learned that secret.

Heading north we touched Fort Worth which was then a small fort up on the bluffs. There was a lively trading post at this point operated by York and Draper, from whom we purchased supplies.

The next sign of habitation was the Red River Station. This was some eight miles east of the present city of Terral, Oklahoma, and about eighty miles west of Sherman, Texas. We obtained badly needed supplies at the Station and headed for the crossing near the mouth of Salt Creek which flowed in from the north.

Thawing snow in the mountains caused high water. We experienced considerable trouble trying to force the cattle into the cold current. Soon a couple of waddies rode out from the Station to assist. We hurrahed the cattle down the steep incline into the river and then forced our horses in, keeping on the downstream side of the herd. This stopped the milling and got the leaders started across. I had heard of "water founder" and thought it meant too much water, which would make the cattle sick. It also meant "fear of water and refusal to cross." Once cattle get into that habit it is nearly impossible to break. After we learned to swim on the downstream side of the cattle we had no more trouble. They never turn upstream to "mill," but always downstream, and once they turn it is nearly impossible to keep them from going back the way they came.

As soon as the opposite bank had been gained we started for the highlands where it was easier to manage them. Having crossed the Red, we had left Texas and entered Indian Territory.

Chapter Seven

Crossing Indian Territory

About twenty-five miles north of the Red River crossing we came upon a very prominent eminence known as Monument Hill, atop which were two stone markers, perhaps three hundred feet apart. It was said the cowboys heaped up these rocks, making a pile some ten or twelve feet high and about as thick. They could be seen from a distance of six or eight miles from most any direction. Passing herders scratched their names into the soft stone. It was an interesting autograph album and had it been saved would have been a wonderful historic relic. But when the trail was abandoned the settlers hauled away the rocks and soon all evidence of the monuments disappeared.

The rivers of the I.T. and southern Kansas were generally sandy and their bottoms were quicksand. The streams were all subject to sudden floods which kept the bottoms stirred up and soft. It was never safe to go across without first testing the fords.

Horses with their large feet could travel the treacherous bottoms pretty good, but once they started to sink down their large hoofs were harder to pull free and consequently losses were heavy. Mules with their smaller hoofs fared better.

If it was possible to put the cattle across first, it was always done. Their cloven hoofs spread out and supported their weight. On the other hand, if they got into quicksand they were better able to withdraw their feet as their hoofs would contract and offer less suction.

I think the crossings of the Salt Fork of the Cimarron and the South Canadian were the worst and the most feared on the Trail, seconded only by the Boggy, which richly deserved that name. The Red River and the North Canadian were about as nasty. More time was spent pulling cattle out of those waters than all the rest of our troubles combined.

In the northern reaches of the I.T., Pond Creek and Pond Lake was another set of troublemakers. Some twenty-five miles west were salt marshes and swamps. Indians went to these salt marshes for the supply of that essential element. Our Boss was trail wise and he shoved us two or three miles east of the junction of Pond and Osage Creek just above the Salt Fork. These tributaries formed a large loop and made a natural swamp or lake (Pond Lake) which was fed by the brackish waters to the west. It was a bog, if ever there was a bog, and in addition to this, the water was so bad it was nearly poison for the cattle to drink.

I think the largest prairie dog town I ever saw was in that section of the country. Before reaching Pond Creek we traveled at least twenty-five miles through a colony of prairie dogs, owls, rattlesnakes, and buzzards. The highlands were all infested with these pests.

However, old Mother Nature was not always parsimonious. At Caddo Spring a large flow of pure water gushed from the ground. Everything was lovely there except for the two graves not far from the springs. The story was that two cowboys had been overtaken by a raiding band of Indians and killed. This happened but a few months prior to our drive. It was a stern warning to us and we earned our name of "bush-poppers" as we hurried out of that country.

While the Osage Indians were on the reservation and were supposed to be civilized, that status was hardly skin deep. They claimed they never went on the warpath but what they did was about as bad. The Osage people believed a dead warrior must have scalps to his credit, else he would never inherit the glories of the Happy Hunting Grounds. Consequently if a warrior died without first having secured an enemy scalp one or two of his friends were obliged to go out and get some. The scalps were then buried with the deceased, thus insuring him a future life of companionship with his fellow heathens. These solicitous friends called themselves "funeral parties" or "mourning parties," never war parties. So these two cowboys at Caddo Springs, as well as settlers who came in later, were killed by "friendly Indians" as a religious rite.

Chapter Eight

Trail Lingo

As we traveled across the Indian Territory, or I.T. as it was more commonly designated, we ran upon some buffalo. Only a few years previously this region had been literally covered with them but now they had been killed off or they had been driven westward.

We could appreciate the extent of the buffalo traffic. Huge piles of their hides were waiting shipment at all railroad stations in Kansas and Nebraska when we arrived there. I marveled at the quantity, but was told they represented but a drop in the bucket compared to what was coming into the stations a hundred miles west.

The killers now had a well-regulated system. They no longer killed for the hides only, but for the meat as well. It was no longer possible to take one's gun and after a few hours hunting bring in a supply of meat. They now went a long distance from town. The meat was saved by cutting it in long strips and letting it sun dry before salt packing it in barrels. The hides were dried and baled and hauled to the nearest railroad for shipment to the various tanneries.

I saw several outfits all rigged out for hunting. Three yoke of oxen were hitched to two large wagons that were coupled with short poles and driven by one man. They traveled in convoys of several units. When they came to a bad place which they could not negotiate they uncoupled the wagons and took out one load at a time.

Along the way we noticed many circular spots of various dimensions, ranging from thirty feet to a hundred feet in diameter. As a rule they were nearly round. An old buffalo hunter told me they were "buffalo rings." They were trampled in the grass where the salty old bulls had traveled in circles around the females of the herd and their calves. This was done in order to fight away prowling animals who would tear down the calves. Any time the herd was threatened the cows would always face outward, which put the little ones in a hollow behind them. At the same time the old fellows would go raging and tearing around the herd, looking for the prowler.

In every drive there were always a few lazy cattle and also some footsore critters which we called "drags." It was necessary to control the movement of the herd to the gait of the drags, which made the "drifting" method the most efficient. When the cattle got too footsore to travel, they were dropped. Sometimes the Lobos got them, and again it might be the Indians, who were always on the lookout for such pickings regardless of how thin. Occasionally the strays found their way into later drives which came up the trail. In that case the road-brand would denote ownership and the proceeds of the sale would go to the rightful owner. Maybe.

As the herd neared water the "leaders" and stronger animals would strike out but as the trail boss had anticipated this, they were widely scattered and consequently all would not reach water at the same time. The leaders could then drink without being crowded and it kept the herd from tromping the waterhole. At many points the waterholes were merely large ponds, or small creeks, all with mud bottoms. It did not take much tromping to turn them into mudholes which would be worthless by the time the "drags" reached it.

In the early days a man named Samuel Maverick was an early Texas rancher. As time went on he acquired thousands upon thousands of acres of land. His range was divided into ranches. One of the smaller units was in charge of a man who was instructed to brand all calves that came from his original four hundred cows. He was too lazy to do the branding. However, his neighbors respected Maverick's un-branded calves and let them run inasmuch as everything else was branded. Whenever the stockmen came to an unbranded animal, they would say: "That belongs to Maverick." It was not long until the word began to be applied by cowboys and stockmen to all unbranded stock.

I have been asked what was a dogie. Dogies were unfortunate calves whose mothers have died and whose fathers have eloped with the other cows.

Chapter Nine

Cowboy, Cowpoke, Cowpuncher

The word that amused me the most was "bush-poppers." This was coined for the boys that worked the mesquite and scrub country and is easy to define. It was applied to the waddies who "tailed" the cattle in the thickets or endeavored to pop them out into the open.

The origin of names is an interesting thought. I don't know where the name "waddy" came from, but perhaps from the peculiar walk or waddle of the knight of the saddle. The moniker "herder" smacks of the Mid-west small farm, and the polite expression "cowboy" carries the refinement of the Easterner. One is safe in saying Texas was the beginning of both the cattle ranches and the cowboy. Their customs and expressions were brought up the trail to the northern ranges. Down in Texas the word "cowboy" is seldom used, and then it applies to the younger boys. It was told the name started during the Civil War when the older men were away and the lads were left to herd the cattle. Further north, the word "cowboy" is in general usage, as is the word "peeler." It was not safe to call a man a peeler in certain parts of the South as the word was more commonly used for card sharps and swindlers.

The adult riders were more commonly known as "pokes" and "cowpokes." Later the word "puncher" seemed to be more generally used. The truth is, both "cowpokes" and "cowpunchers" are of similar origin with "cowpoke" first being a Texas word while I think "puncher" is a Western adaptation. The names were applied to the men who were caretakers on the cattle trains. You would see them carry the long poles with the sharp points, and every time the train stopped they hustled down the line of cars to punch up the downers and level out the load.[1]

Anyway, we think the word "puncher" is derived from the adjective "poke" (descriptive of a rider). That is pretty complicated reasoning, so if you don't understand my explanation you will have to go down there and they will demonstrate to you how a "poke" plays poker. The Texans claim poker is a gentleman's game and is as essential as his breath. It is the only activity a man should indulge in other than hunting. The Texans also claim, and they don't bat an eye when they do it, they are the nation, while the rest of the states are merely ticks hanging on, which accounts for the game of poker being called the national game.

The super-ultima of poker playing is to spread a blanket on the ground and play in the light of the trail fire. The stakes may be anything from a dime to a man's horse, or it may be the owner's entire herd of cattle. I saw a large ranch change ownership on the turn of a card—and more than one herd has changed hands over a gambling table. But in the end, all winners were losers, for they usually left the wad with the girls and gold-brick artists.

There is one article I never saw pledged, and that was a waddy's saddle. His saddle is the emblem of his trade, and in a manner his most sacred possession. Once a saddle is broken in to fit the contours of one's body it is an unreplaceable piece of property. The saying is that a poke will walk home carrying his saddle but without his pants—rather than walk home in the finest suit of clothes, but without his saddle.

Chapter Ten
Six Inches to Hell

Our cook shack was an old style wagon. I don't suppose you would know what I meant if I called them "linch-pin" wagons. Instead of a hubcap screwed on the axle to hold the wheels, a large pin was passed through the axle. Otherwise, the outfit was about the same as later day ones.

Every cook had his oddities and every set of cowboys were a little different. Once we arrived on the Plains we passed over hundreds of miles of trail with but little or no wood, and that wood was to be found on the streams. We tied a couple of large logs on each side of the chuck wagon and these were used for two purposes: to help float the outfit across swollen streams, and it was also an ace in the hole when we ran out of firewood. The only trouble was the cook usually picked on some of us to help split logs, which didn't go so well, but we didn't dare refuse. The old slum-thrower could get even by cutting down on our dried apples.

As we came up the Trail, we swung wide of Wichita, leaving the herd to pasture the cattle on Chisholm Creek while we took in the town. Afterwards we moved on and things went smooth enough. A day's drive north of Wichita we came to a small jumping off place called Sedgwick, which was just a section house and a few shacks where the gandies lived.

We did not see a person or a house for the next ninety miles. The steers were rattling off the distance in a jaunty manner and the waddies put on their "before Christmas manners" in the hopes the Boss would give an extra day at Abilene. We were anxious to know if the town was deserving of its reputation—'twas said it was six hundred feet down to water and six inches to hell. We found very little water. The old scout did not let us down. While yet some twenty miles distant he told four of us to accompany him in search of good pasture in which to lay over. The balance of the pokes had to swallow their disappointment while they trailed behind.

The spring of 1871 found me at Abilene. Once there we were met by an agent from the McCoy stockyards whose business it was to assign grazing grounds to incoming strings.¹ The herd moved up and with old man Ware's longhorns safe behind feedyard gates we were left free to proceed with the celebration and, believe me, the boys sure did. It was the first opportunity to cut the alkali in their throats and it took a mighty strong potion to do it and a lot of the stuff. Their whistles were all dry and needed a right smart lubrication while our lips were so parched, cracked, and encrusted with trail dust that we couldn't grin and it was painful to talk.

We hit the barbershop first, where a few layers of dirt peeled off with the whiskers. By the time we had been roached, taken baths, and purchased new bandanas for our necks our appearances were so altered it was hard to recognize old friends. Pay in our pockets and pockets in our pants, we whistled in the dog and gave the whole works a rousing damn. Some of the boys proceeded to paint the town red while others decided it should go prohibition and attempted to drink it dry. I did not care for that sort of thing so I spent my time looking around and when it was all over I had saved most of my money and had a great store of interesting memories while the gang had headaches and were busted.

Home and mother's mince pie was uppermost in our minds as each solemnly vowed "niver agin, so help me Calamity Jane!" That night Ware herded us into a bunkhouse, the first we had entered in many months. We did our best to bed down on the shuck mattress but it was no go. My partner was the first to stampede. He complained bitterly about the bump mattress, and that his feet were too warm. I told him to take off his boots. He jumped the bedding grounds and located a spot in the yard where he stretched out on the ground with his head cradled on his saddle and his boots at the side. The old hoss blanket was pulled over his ears to keep away the skeeters, but the little devils snooked through the worn spots and got in their dirty work. However, he was soon asleep and snorting vehemently.

Come morning we shook the dew and waited for the sun to break through the river mists. At last the red disk broke through and she came up in the right direction for us—east. That pointed toward home and home folks and thinking about it made me more homesick than any past experience. However, the breakfast bell knocked sentimental thoughts gaily west. It was time to be practical.

As we polished leather that morning I got to thinking about the old world being like a fractious horse. She had to be rode, come rain or high water. If you get dumped, just get up, pull out the stickers, and climb back on. Every hoss can be broken to ride—it just takes plenty of intestinal fortitude.

There is a cowboy song [see "Cowboy Songs and Verses"] that relates to this—

> "If a feller's been a straddle,
> since he's big enough to ride,
> And has had to sling his saddle on
> most any colored hide,
> Though it's nothing to take pride in,
> still most fellers I have knowed,
> If they ever done much ridin', has at
> different times got throwed.
> Moppin' up the canyon's surface with
> the bosom of your pants,
> Then you get up on your trotters,
> but you have a job to stand;
> For the landscape 'round you totters
> and your collar's full of sand.

> Lots of fellers give you the prescription
>   how a broncho should be rode,
>   But there's few that give description
>   of the time when they got throwed."

Chapter Eleven

The Murder of Marshal Smith

The new marshal of Abilene was "Wild Bill" Hickok, the late Marshal Tom Smith having been killed a few months prior to our arrival. The law had been getting the better of the outlaws, cattle rustlers, and common variety of Texas punchers who figured they had to stand the city on end and they were never satisfied until they had given it a grand hurrah—in other words, chased the marshal out of town, shot up the city, and taken possession in general. A marshal was lucky to leave with his life. The fact is several officers had been killed before Smith took over the office. As soon as the rowdy element learned a new officer was on the job they started to hurrah the town.

The ringleader was a huge fellow known as "Big Jeff." He was a dangerous man at anytime, a known killer, and when intoxicated he was a person to avoid. As Big Jeff came down the street with both guns popping and his mouth emitting war-whoops every person scuttled for cover and Jeff soon had the street to himself. It was then Marshal Smith walked out to meet Big Jeff. The first thing Jeff said was to demand that Smith scamper for the cactus or get killed. Smith stood his ground, with both hands free. Each man was waiting for the other to make a break for his gun.

Big Jeff told Smith he and his gang intended to hurrah the town when they pleased, and they refused to park their guns according to the rule. Smith told Jeff to shut up and to turn in his gun. As he talked his steely eyes bored into Big Jeff and Jeff slowly backed away. At last Smith saw his opportunity and "buffaloed" Jeff. The big bully dropped as though hit with an ax. He was expecting Smith to use a gun. Instead Smith swung with his fist. When Jeff tried to get up he was knocked flat again and again and at last was hauled to the police court where he was fined $25.00 and costs.

To be buffaloed is the worst disgrace that can happen to a gunman—but it sure had a wonderful effect on the crowd. After that there was no trouble getting the men to register their guns as they entered town. It was either that or ride out of town in a lumber wagon headed for the cemetery.

In October 1870 Andrew McConnell shot and killed John Shea. It seems Shea snapped a pistol twice at McConnell and was cocking his gun the third time when Andy went into action and killed Shea. Investigation exonerated McConnell. Farmer neighbors of Shea's demanded a trial—without doubt it was the usual quarrel between the overbearing cowboys and the settlers.

A warrant was issued for McConnell and a man named Moses Miles. Smith, with two deputies, went out to arrest the men who were living in a cut-bank on Chapman Creek. Without warning McConnell shot Smith. A tussle ensued and while the wounded Smith was putting the handcuffs on McConnell, Miles came around and picked up an ax and nearly cut off Smith's head. Smith's deputies had skedaddled at the first shot and they soon reached town with the news.

I think it was November that Smith was killed. Feeling ran high and the people demanded a stop to the lawless element.[1] Smith had been able to hold them down, but a certain element of the townsmen who profited by the lawless element kept things agitated. Smith was well liked, he had a fine personality, he was absolutely honest, and even the outlaws respected his authority. He never killed except in self-defense, but he was a past master at the "buffalo" game.

On the other hand, "Wild Bill" Hickok was a killer. He shot first and talked afterwards. I knew him well. He was a sulky sort of a fellow, an arrogant cuss, overbearing, and he took every opportunity to feather his own nest.

Chapter Twelve
Eyes Like Gimlets

As we stayed over in Abilene the outfit was rigged out and the cook's stores replenished. [1] It was here that I saw "Arkansas" as he too had come up the trail with a herd of cattle. Previously our paths had crossed as I was working my way around Texas. He was a small, nervous acting, highly strung man, and his eyes were like gimlets. When I had first met him he was known as a killer and as a badman, although his reputation was yet under construction. His hands and fingers moved like lightning as he dealt cards and those hands knew every trick of the game. If one made an accusing remark that was not backed up with a six-gun he was very apt to read his own obituary next morning while he cooled his heels awaiting admittance to the lower regions.

I had heard of Arkansas being John Wesley Hardin but it was not generally known. Although I had recognized him, I pretended otherwise and awaited his pleasure to admit a previous acquaintance. It was mighty lucky for me I held my tongue. A new hotel was being built, known as the Cottage Hotel. [2] While we were in Abilene the building was getting used, although it was still being worked on. Curtains were used as partitions and to cover some of the doorways. One of the punchers became liquored up and then his tongue began to wag. What he said was not at all favorable to Arkansas and it was very evident he knew the man as Hardin and was going to "talk." Fear of disclosure caused Arkansas to shoot the cowboy in cold blood in the hotel. Ark jumped through a window like a turpentined cat and escaped.

At the edge of town the railroad operated their stockyards. Nearby a man of shady repute conducted a public corral. The punchers would leave their horses with him. He pastured them out on the prairie and penned them in the yards at night. This was cheaper than putting up at the livery stable. Besides it was to the liking of certain characters who could come and go without too much notice.

Arkansas helped himself to one of these horses, but first he told the manager he was in a hurry and if there was any talking there would be another man for Boot Hill, but if he acted sensible and kept mum, the hoss would be returned before long. The escape was complete and no more was heard of Arkansas, although the horse was returned to Abilene.

Several years after Abilene, Hardin's father-in-law lived at Austin. Neither he nor his wife could read or write. A lawman there, without letting these people know who he was, gained their confidence and he read a letter Hardin wrote them. There was a large reward out for the arrest of Arkansas and it was well worthwhile to work on the case.

At last the marshal was able to locate Hardin. He and two deputies went after the man. They knew better than to go alone and they went prepared for trouble. It seems Hardin had decided to move at that particular time and it so happened the train he boarded was the same train the officers were on. They recognized Hardin and then waited for him to set down. Then two of the men found a seat directly behind him. Later the marshal entered the car and when opposite Hardin he poked his gun in the man's face. Hardin did not intend to be taken that easy and started for his guns but the two men back of him grabbed his arms and he was soon handcuffed.

I was at Austin in late 1877 at the time Hardin was returned there for safe keeping in that jail. While I had known Arkansas some six years earlier, it still rankled in my mind whether Hardin was the same man. After reading of his arrest I decided to satisfy my curiosity and went to the county building where I explained to the sheriff my reasons and asked if I could identify the man. The request was granted and before long I was looking at Hardin and recognized my old time friend Arkansas. There were many accusations of murder against him. I left the next day and did not learn what was done [see "John Wesley Hardin"].

Chapter Thirteen
Wild Bill Hickok

Wild Bill was ruling the roost when we came to Abilene. There were three places we could register our guns: with the sheriff, at the saloons, or at the livery barn. Once the men got in the habit, they saw that every newcomer did likewise and in this manner they played in with the law. It was not so much that they loved the sheriff as it was self-preservation. They positively refused to permit others to roam around with a gun while they themselves were unarmed.

One evening I saw Wild Bill arrest a man who was standing beside me in the saloon. He had wanted to arrest the same man a month before over some minor affair which should have been overlooked. The man left town but returned a month later. This time he had a lot of money. I know I was staggered at the size of the roll he displayed, and I was amazed that he should do such a thing. Wild Bill kept in the background. He let the man load up and when he was pretty well soused, Bill cracked him an unmerciful rap on the head with his Colt. The poor fellow fell like a pooled beef and was knocked out colder than a mackerel. Bill and a couple of deputies hauled the victim out into the street and in a few minutes they carried him up to the jail. When he came out of the jail he came out without his money. It's your guess what happened.

Chapter Fourteen
Buffaloing

I have used the word "buffalo" several times. Just where it came from I never learned, but the term was used when a man was knocked out, in particular, when a sheriff bent his gun barrel over a man's head, the most effective way to handle a bully. In later years an officer used a "sap" or a "billy" but in the wild and wooly days he would have been killed while going for a billy. Consequently, he used his gun. I have seen movies of an officer in the act of buffaloing an offender and they show him holding the barrel of the gun in his hand while he conked the man with the handle of the gun. To have clubbed a man that way would have been sheer suicide. There is not a man living who is fast enough to switch ends with his gun and then go into action. The offender, as a rule, was a badman; he was armed and he would have shot the sheriff long before he could have acted effectively.

I do not think Wild Bill ever buffaloed a badman; that was not his method. He preferred to shoot. However, in later years while at Dodge City, I did see Wyatt Earp buffalo an armed man who was reaching for his gun. If you do not think a 10-inch .45 caliber barrel will do the job, you just try it. More than one skull has been seriously cracked without striking very hard.

The Indians used the word "buffalo" when speaking of the Negro soldiers. They were amazed when they first saw their kinky hair and as they always used descriptive words, they likened the men to a buffalo's head, which had curly hair. Thereafter the soldiers were known as buffalo soldiers. Of course this has nothing to do with the method of buffaloing which has just been explained.

Chapter Fifteen

Wild Bill and the Tinhorn Gamblers

A tinhorn gambler by the name of Red worked in the saloon where Wild Bill hung out. Of course Red had a confederate but no one was supposed to know it. I had been watching Red a day or two and enjoyed the slick way he worked. One day a cowboy named Sandy came in from the trail and as usual he had been paid off. This young bucka-roo came swaggering into the saloon and up to the bar for a drink. He wanted to talk and it was not long before he was engaged in conversation with the gambler.

Red pretended to know all about Sandy's friends. He did it by making leading remarks after Sandy had spun a yarn. Sandy fell for his new acquaintance like a ton of brick. At last the gambler asked Sandy to drink for the sake of old friends and associations—and they proceeded to liquor up. In the meantime Red's accomplice Butch entered the saloon and it seemed he too knew some of Sandy's friends, although he pretended to be a stranger to Red.

The drinks were passed again. Red started to pay for them but Butch insisted on paying and before long the two men were quarreling about it. The bartender settled the dispute by suggesting they throw dice to see who paid. The first throw the drinks were on Red. They threw for another round of drinks and this time Red won. Then he wanted to bet Butch he could guess the number that would come up by throwing three's. They bet a dollar and Red won. Sandy was an interested spectator. They then threw again and Red said it would be a 21. He won his throw also. Thereafter Red bet on the 21 while Butch would select some other number and he lost on every throw. Butch left in disgust. In the meantime Red had whispered to Sandy that the dice were loaded, that was why the number 21 always came up.[1]

Red went over to a table and sat down to a poker game. He had no sooner settled down than here comes Butch, all hot and heavy for another game of dice tossin'. Red held off long enough for Butch and Sandy to get anxious. Then he quit the poker game and the three went over to the bar.

Butch announced he had $50.00 that said he could guess the next throw and he called his number. Red called the bet, but when he went into his breeches he pretended to discover he did not have enough money to cover. Sandy took the hook and tossed down $50.00 for Red—and when the bones came rattling out of the cup, up came the number Butch had called. Sandy did not know that Red had changed the dice on him.

Red and Butch immediately left the saloon and it was several seconds before Sandy realized he had been taken for a ride. He then

rushed over to Wild Bill who had been watching the game and demanded that both men be arrested for fraud. Wild Bill went rushing
out and after a bit he returned with a man in custody.

It was sure a comedy to see the expression on Sandy's face when
he saw the man Bill had apprehended. He was a Dutchman who had
never been in the saloon, but who had come to town to do a little
shopping and was in the act of hitching up when Wild Bill poked a
gun in his ribs and demanded his surrender. The man could not talk
English. All he could say was "Mein Gott, Mein Gott." Sandy howled,
"You so-and-so, that ain't the man."

After some argument Bill released the sputtering Dutchman and
went out in search of the crooks, but of course never found them. He
did not intend to find Red and Butch. He pulled the stall of arresting
the Dutchman in order to give the sharpers time to escape. Sandy
knew the marshal had seen the play, but there was nothing to be done
and he knew better than to call Bill's hand. Such tricks were pulled
right along and Wild Bill seemed to play in with the gang.

Hickok killed a saloon-keeper who had come up the trail with some
cattle from Austin, Texas. The man became drunk and offensive. He
was notified to get out of town but his reply was that of a stupidly
drunk man and should have been considered in that light. The man
came down the middle of the street, and it took all of the street as his
feet were prone to travel this way and that way. Anyone seeing the man
knew he was harmless even though he carried a gun in his hand. He
was too cockeyed to use it. Of course he was violating the rule as no
guns were allowed to be toted in town and he threatened the marshal,
which was chatter from a thick tongue.

Had it been Marshal Smith the man would have been buffaloed.
Instead, Wild Bill placed himself at the corner of a building and waited
for the parade. When the man got within fair range Bill blasted him
with slugs from his .45 without giving the victim a warning or attempting to make an arrest. Of course he killed the man deader than
a nit. This was generally considered to be the beginning of the end
of Wild Bill. He had made some deadly enemies and sooner or later

he was bound to walk into a peck of trouble, which he did. He went to Deadwood and there met his own untimely end at the hands of an avenging friend of the murdered saloon-keeper [see "The Death of Hickok"].

Chapter Sixteen

Trouble in Nebraska

Moving on to the Nebraska feedyards, we found there were no improvements north of Abilene until we hit the Republican River country.[1] This we followed north for some distance until we were ready to jump across to Rose Creek where Thompson, Nebraska, now stands.[2]

The trail north of Abilene was new with the paths being scattered. In many places we made our own trail as the Boss rode ahead to spot out the way. It was necessary that water be no farther than a day's drive. We averaged ten to twelve miles each day, but there were times we had to force the herd twenty miles or more to reach water.

Nebraska had passed a law prohibiting cattle from entering the state from the South after frost in the Spring and before frost in the Fall. I believe the reason was to keep out the Texas fever. At that time they did not know it was the tick that caused the trouble, but they did know cold weather stopped it.

Ware wished to beat this law. Finding ourselves in camp just below the border we had to make a very early morning start in order to get into Nebraska before the farmers knew what was going on. Once in the state we would be alright. We expected trouble anyway as Mr. Ware had become involved over the question of trespass on a previous trip.

The farmers became very hostile when they saw Texas cattle and I do not blame them for their attitude. Some of their stock had become infected with the fever and considerable loss sustained. It was rather amusing to see the women, children, and men rush out after their cattle and shoo them away as they saw our herd approach.

We crossed Rose Creek just as dawn was breaking and by the time it was light we were several miles inside the line. A friendly farmer permitted us to water and feed our cattle. Because of the early start we did not have breakfast, so with the cattle fed and watered the cook proceeded to make camp and start a fire. But before doing so we hacked down the tall grass and cleared away a good spot for the fire. There was a high wind blowing and we did not wish to take chances of starting a prairie fire.

With our campfire going, we settled down for a bite to eat when a gust of wind caught up a bunch of burning grass which had been twisted into rope and carried it into the heavier grass. It was but a moment until the entire works went up in a flash.[3] We did all we could to smother the fire, but it was out of control from the start. Nearby were two large stacks of feed. These were soon a flaming mass. Ware later settled with that farmer for the hay and damages. Out on the prairie was another homesteader who had a straw stable and a sod house. The stable and a horse burned.[4]

The fire raged all night and the reflection of the flames lighted the skies and ground sufficiently for one to read a paper. The wind-swept fire jumped the Little Blue and then burned across to the Big Blue, and the Lord only knows what would have been next had not a heavy rain came up mid-afternoon.[5]

Next day we kept the herd moving while Mr. Ware settled some of the fire bills. Later a sheriff came out from Fairbury and served a warrant on the nine of us for starting the fire and causing damages. We had to return to Fairbury for trial.[6] The time was set for 3 PM but we were late getting there as the rain had turned to snow and the muddy trails were very bad. The prosecuting attorney was going to hang it on us for being late, but the Justice of the Peace before whom the hearing was held was a good old sport. He ruled that it was three o'clock until it was four o'clock, and then ordered the trial to proceed. Our lawyer advised us to keep quiet, say nothing, and swear to nothing. They had no witnesses to the start of the fire and therefore they would be unable to prove anything against us. This turned out to be the fact and the jury gave us a verdict of "not guilty."

From Fairbury the herd moved to Beatrice and thence on to the Peru bottoms where they ranged for a short time before going on to Nebraska City. Mr. Ware was a cattle feeder but he could not get this bunch of slabsided longhorns to eat. They didn't know what corn was and darned if they cared to learn. Even after some of them did get to eating grain they did not put on gain fast enough to pay. That bunch of 250 longhorns along with the trail expenses and the trouble caused by the fire busted old man Ware flatter than a mackerel.[7] [See "The Prairie Fire" and "The Abilene Market Crash"]

Part Two

Over the Western Trail, 1878

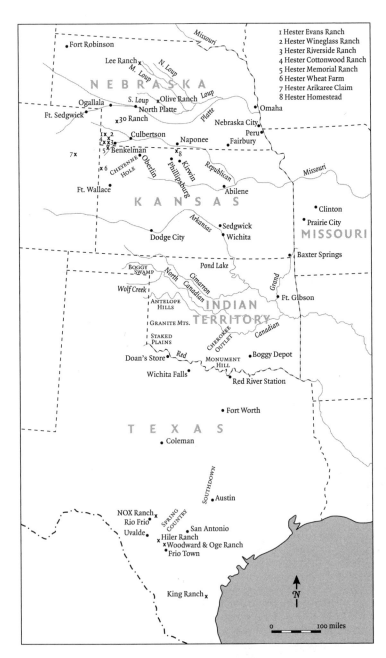

1 Hester Evans Ranch
2 Hester Wineglass Ranch
3 Hester Riverside Ranch
4 Hester Cottonwood Ranch
5 Hester Memorial Ranch
6 Hester Wheat Farm
7 Hester Arikaree Claim
8 Hester Homestead

Map of Places Mentioned

Chapter Seventeen
Back in Texas

As the years passed my calluses wore down and saddle sores disappeared. In a like ratio so too did my memory of trail hardships fade away. Within a short time I found myself watching the setting sun and wondering what laid over that way. Surely something of great interest!

I do not recall when I first heard Professor Dale's description of a pioneer stockman, perhaps in later years, but his words vividly portray the story—"A kind of twilight zone; with the light of civilization behind and the darkness of savagery before."[1]

There was something about "twilight" which took the sting from the memory of a blistering sun; and the words "light of civilization" was a challenge to most any aspiring bush-popper. Then and there I decided the world was my bacon and it was time to put it in my frying pan. Incidentally, I forgot the vows of '71 and Dad's earlier admonition, "Whupping the world is like having a bull by the tail. He kin travel faster than 'ary a man, so hang on kid or he'll get you."

There was an old cowboy song that echoed my sentiments at the time—

> 'Twas good to live when all was sod,
> Without no fences and no fuss;
> Belonging in partnership with God,
> the government, and us

God gave my brother Elmer the brains and me the fat and itchy feet.[2] Consequently I was not at all surprised to find myself headed for Texas in company with several would-be cow waddies of the Iowa variety. The first day's travel was uneventful, but I do recall a most astonishing revelation. I re-discovered why cowboys "walk that way."

The winter of 1877–78 was spent partially in Uvalde country. This is the home of our vice-president, John Nance Garner.[3] The balance of the time was frittered away in both Frio county and the Spring country, with my headquarters in a dobie town named Rio Frio. [4] Among that winter's accomplishment was a rich fund of Mexican cuss words, which I never used, and a taste for tamales, which I tried to satisfy.

One of the most important ranches on the Frio River, near Rio Frio, was the NOX brand operated by Meyers and Roberts. I warmed saddle for them during part of the fall cow-hunt and helped brand calves. We were sent out two by two to work the calves where found. A running iron was used instead of the present type of letter branding. The running iron was a slower method of applying a brand but at that time large brands were applied and it would have been nearly impossible to carry lettered irons of that size. Another outfit was the Woodward and Oge in Frio County [see "The Ranches of '78"]. [5]

I noticed a great improvement in the quality of the cattle between 1871 and 1877. Easterners had brought shorthorns with their emigrant trains. These had been crossed with the natives. Then there were the Herefords, which were imported into Texas by a doctor in 1875. He brought in three fine cows and a registered sire. The sire and two cows died of Spanish fever before spring. The remaining cow dropped a calf and by the following spring both the cow and calf had died. When I first hit the Trail in '71 no one mentioned Herefords, but in '77 there was plenty of talk as the last of the doctor's Herefords had just died. The news spread all over the country. It was not long before more Herefords were introduced and from then on the improvement was rapid.

Chapter Eighteen

Cow Chow

When I first went over the Chisholm Trail in 1871 there was a very common bush called the buffalo pea. This bush was about eighteen inches high and branched out a foot or so in width. It was a very prolific producer and was covered with small pods about three inches long. The pods were full of small peas. The buffalo was very fond of them and in eating the pea many of the seeds dropped to the ground where they sprouted and grew. But as the cattle began to range the country they went right after the pea and not only did they eat all the pods on the vine, but they licked the ground clean. In a very short time the buffalo pea disappeared and as far as I know, they never came back. One might say the buffalo pea went the way of the buffalo.

The range and grazing lands of that part of Texas were covered with a mesquite grass, a wiry affair similar to our own Republican River alkali or salt grass. It grew about six inches high and while yet green was fairly decent forage, but with fall the top turned brittle and there was little nutrition left. Between the ticks, fever, and scanty range, the cattle had a tough time of it, almost as tough as they themselves.

The broad-leaf cactus was very common. It would grow six to eight feet high and the leaves were as large as one's hand, up to double that size. Like most cacti it was covered with spikes. Some cattle got to eating the leaves, but the spikes soon caused festered mouths and before long the poor critters starved to death. In the early days of Nebraska the homesteaders fed common cactus in the winter, but first the spikes were broken down and singed. Even at that there were sore mouths and some mortality. About all you can say for the practice, it beat eating a snow bank.

Then too there was a mesquite bush or tree. Some of the peelers called them the Devil's Thorn. It grew very rank and thickly covered the infected territory. The trunks were from four to twelve inches in diameter and as high as twelve to eighteen feet. The mesquite was covered with nasty sharp thorns and when ridden into we knew the Devil was on the job. They carried a pretty bloom, and fruited with clusters of a bean-like seed which made rich horse feed. I believe they ripened in early summer. The bush-poppers wore heavy cow-hide chaparejos, leather packets, cuffs, and gloves when working in the mesquite brush. Otherwise we would have been literally cut to ribbons.

Chapter Nineteen

Mr. Hiler

Mr. Hiler went to Texas in 1853—that was the year I was born—not that my birthday had anything to do with it, but it did set the date in my mind.[1] When he arrived his worldly possessions amounted to a wife, three children, a team and wagon, and fifty cents in cash. In 1877 he paid taxes on an assessed valuation of $125,000.00.

I asked him how he got his start. His reply was about as follows: "The Texas Republic declared early on all unbranded cattle were public property. The Declaration continued as an unwritten law when she became a state. Any critter over a year old which was not branded was considered a maverick (without ownership) and the person who applied his own brand upon this animal became the owner. The branding of such a critter could not be questioned and it established ownership, even though the true origin was known."[2]

Mr. Hiler worked hard and rode far. Few mavericks escaped his rope and once snared they had a new home. In time he accumulated a large herd, many of them raised at the other man's expense, while he himself imported shorthorns for crossbreeding. Even though the cattle were cheap, when sold they purchased cheap land and as the years passed Hiler waxed mighty in the realm, and as Abraham of old, he could sit in his tent door and see his thousands of kine upon his many hillsides.[3]

The King Ranch was the largest in Texas and was over thirty-five miles across. The King brand was the "Running W" and it was known from the Rio Grande to Montana.[4] One day while riding with Mr. King upon King's domain, Hiler saw an unbranded past-yearling steer which was still sucking its mother, although she also had a two-day-old calf at her side. The mother carried the Running W and there was no question but that all three cattle belonged to King. However, Mr. Hiler told me he tossed his lariat over the older nursing steer and proceeded to apply the Hiler brand while the rightful owner looked on, as pleasant as you please, and he seemed rather amused. Perhaps King recalled to mind the many times he himself had done the same trick.[5]

The cattle were all pasture bred and as a rule the old cow weaned her calf come fall. Believe me she could wean a calf mighty quick. Those long, sharp horns soon convinced the calf to move on. But occasionally there was one who refused to be weaned regardless of the punishment, or there was a cow that would not fight the calf away. In either event there was not sufficient milk for a second, newly dropped calf, and being the weaker it soon starved.

Just another tragedy of the plains.

Chapter Twenty

The Texas Trail

Soon enough, I again hired out as a trail-herder, this time being a top-hand and commanding $40.00 a month in wages plus food.[1] I furnished my own saddle, bridle, horse, and war-bag. Instead of 250 head of steers for the Nebraska feedlots as in 1871, we now trailed 2600 longhorn range stockers—cows and calves—headed for the Loup [see "The Ranches of '78"]. We were eighteen punchers working two by two, instead of nine cow-waddies working to beat hell. By 1878 they had learned to trail large bunches without loss. The handy size was around 2500 head. If many more were to be moved it was more profitable to divide the string.

Our cattle were purchased for a New York syndicate headed by Mr. Lee.[2] The first job was to bunch the trailherd. Rounding up the stock was generally a Mexican's job as the men were exceptionally good at working the bush country. As they popped the cattle out of the chaparral we moved them to a public corral, several of which were scattered in the most convenient round-up centers.

The corrals were constructed of heavy poles set on end and laced together with rawhide. They had to be very high and strong to hold the longhorns. Some of these corrals were huge affairs, perhaps a quarter of a mile across, and had wide wings extending out and away from the opening in order to funnel the nervous cattle towards the gate. Once in, they were sorted, counted, and road brands were applied.

As a rule the Texans preferred the "cut and sort" method where the cattle were held on the prairies and all sorting was done by riding into the main herd, the victim hazed to the outside where other riders shooed it into the trail-bound herd, later to be consolidated with other bunches and at last trail-branded. At first the waddies seemed to consider it a disgrace to use corrals or chutes. (I've been asked if we used branding chutes for our cattle. I do not recall ever seeing a chute.) In any event the range hands soon discarded some of their prejudices and began using the more efficient method of corrals.

After being corralled the livestock were held until hungry and plenty thirsty which made them more manageable. They also became acquainted not only with each other, but with their new surroundings and strange noises. After leaving the public corral they were moved to a large pasture where they were held for a week or ten days, this time becoming accustomed to a "surround" in the open. In other words they were pretty well trail broke before a hoof was set on the trail.

This was a profitable investment as they pushed off with a minimum of trouble and they paced away the miles like old-timers, while other herds which had been tossed together and hi-tailed into strange conditions found themselves in continuous grief from start to finish.

Early March 1878 found us rarin' to go; not only was the herd broke, but we too. With sufficient new grass to sustain life, the Boss gave the sign, we forked our hosses, thumbed our noses at the old camp, and pushed away from the Spring country with the prospect of polishing leather for twelve hundred miles.

Abilene had pulled in the latchstring and turned over the welcome mat several years before and the cattle drives had turned to Newton, some 65 miles south. Her fame was more for the honky-tonks, gambling joints, and down-right-hell than for her cattle shipments. The year 1872 saw the last of the Chisholm Trail north of Newton and it was but a short time until the Trail was closed above the Kansas line altogether. Caldwell then took its turn, which was relatively short-lived. Dodge City, some 120 miles west of Abilene, then sat in the game. She asked for a hand and drew to a royal flush and when the chips were counted she took the jackpot of hides, bones, and cattle, sending the balance of the cattle-town home in a barrel.

Southern Texas cattle still used the lower part of the Chisholm Trail as far north as Elm Creek in Wilson County. Here they swung to the northwest for the western crossings of the Red River. One ford was at the mouth of Mud Creek, but the most famous was Doan's, some fifty miles west of Fort Sill. It was here that C. F. Doan opened a store in 1874, and a post office was established the following year. If I recall rightly the city consisted of two dobie or rock buildings with shingled roofs.

We took the more direct route by going through the mountains and after passing Wichita Falls we went west to Doan's famous crossing.[3] Freshets had swollen the river so we laid up for a few days to rest, repair the outfit, and purchase some grub. At the same time we gave the river an opportunity to recede, which it obligingly did. The bottom was poor, several of our stock mired in the quicksand, and we spent a miserable day pulling them out. It was necessary to rig a tow-line with our lariats to pull the chuck-wagon and supply vehicle across.[4]

Chapter Twenty-One

Custer

Doan's was the last sign of habitation until we reached Dodge City. After Doan's there was a small chain of mountains known as the Panhandles wedged down between the Red River and its North Fork. There was barely room enough to make the ford with the cattle and then pass on up the valley of the Fork. It was similar to entering a gate. After proceeding northward some little distance the valley widened out and finally developed into the Staked Plains, some fifty miles or more to the northwest.

About ninety miles north of the Red River we forded the Washita. Off to the west were the Washita Mountains, later known as the Granites. We had to fight snow flurries and chilly winds the entire distance from the Red crossing. Not far away were the Antelope Hills, and it was near them on the Washita that General Custer had wrapped up a Thanksgiving present for the federated tribes under Satanta, Black Kettle, and Little Raven on November 27, 1868. In bitterly cold weather his command had attacked the villages, destroyed one of them, and set fire to their winter's supply of food and hides. At the same time he captured about nine hundred head of Indian ponies, most of which were killed in order to keep them from again falling into the hands of the Indians. Custer discovered the other villages were preparing to attack so he withdrew his forces to Camp Supply.

The victory was saddened by the loss of Major Elliott and his detachment of seventeen men who were cut off by the Indians and killed on the Washita. I understand this was the same officer who with ten men had previously made the dash from the Forks of the Republican (Benkelman, Neb.) to Fort Sedgwick (Julesburg, Colo.) and returned with important dispatches for General Custer. The country was then alive with hostile Indians.

In this incident prior to the Washita battle, Major Elliott barely missed connecting with Lieutenant Kidder and his party of ten men who had been sent from Sedgwick to General Custer on the Republican Forks. Not knowing Kidder was searching for him, General Custer left the Forks for Fort Sedgwick and he too missed Lieutenant Kidder's command. The result was that Kidder detoured for Fort Wallace and was overtaken by the Indians under Pawnee Killer. In the running battle that ensued Kidder and his ten men lost their lives on Beaver Creek near the Sherman and Cheyenne County line in Kansas. This event with Kidder occurred during 1867 [see "Custer and Hester"].

Chapter Twenty-Two

Run ALong Little Dogie, Run Along

Roughly speaking there were two methods of trailing a herd, each of which had its many variations. Some drivers expected to use the entire summer as they moved toward a fall market, or delivery to the Indian Reservation. To do it this way it was necessary to move by easy stages and follow the best water and grass. Grass fat was the slogan. This was the type of herd I had been with in 1871.

But the larger percent of the cattle were of the stocker and "pilgrim" type and these were put through as fast as consistent with good management, keeping in mind they must hold their weight and arrive in good condition. Ours was of this type in 1878.

We left the bedding ground as soon as it was light enough to see. The boys on the "last watch" pointed them in the right direction and held them from scattering too far while others were at chow and some hazed in the cavvy herd from which our day's war-horses were cut. The first men to finish eating were sent out to relieve the herders. Within an hour all of the waddies were in position and lustily singing "Run Along Little Dogie, Run Along."

As a rule the trail boss rode ahead in order to keep us posted on conditions; how far to water, proximity to other herds, and more especially avoiding buffalo and wild horses. We had no trouble with the latter two, but others did. In earlier years the buffalo question was the most important. They would cause a stampede quicker than anything else. I have heard riders tell of holding their herd hours while the buffalo passed, and with them were deer, antelope, elk, wild horses, along with other cattle, all traveling together.

While I was doing Abilene in 1871 I met up with a quiet sobersides by the name of Barroum from down Uvalde way. It seems they came up the trail some earlier than we and at that time he claimed the country between the Salt Fork and the Arkansas was literally over-run with buffalo. They were drifting forward in great herds and their rumble could be heard before they could be seen.

Barroum said their trail boss went ahead to investigate, taking some of the pokes with him. Their own string of cattle was held back but even at that some of the horses and a few head of cattle drifted into the buffalo herd and were never recovered. Strange thing to hear a poke tell that story and at the same time we all know even the odor of a buffalo will often stampede a herd of cattle. It's just another of them things that make us say "Ain't nature grand!" I believe this poke said he was with one of the Choate and Bennett herds and years later I understand Barroum became one of the partners of that outfit.

At the head of our column rode two "pointers" whose duty it was to guide the herd. Further back, evenly spaced along on each side of the string, were six to eight riders. At the rear of the herd were two or three "tailers" who kept the tail end closed in. They fell heir to all of the "necking"—trail necking, not to be confused with the town kind. The tailers had to kill the newly dropped calves and haze along the drags. Following the cattle was the cavvy herd in the charge of two or three wranglers and back of the horses came the chuck-wagon and the supply wagon which carried our sleeping outfit as well as spare parts and extra grub.

If all went favorable, the chuck-wagon would pull ahead and set up camp where the Boss planned to rest the string. By the time we caught up the meal would be ready and the men took turns at the tail end of the chuck-wagon. In this manner there was no lost time and the herd was always well protected.

Come night the horses were run into a lariat-rope corral, or cavvy yard.[1] Two or three men usually rode night guard until the horses were well broke in, then one man sufficed. Perhaps it may sound strange, but a rope laid on the ground was as good as a barb-wire fence. The horses seemed afraid to step over it. However, if suddenly frightened they might bolt over it, hence the night guard.

To provide against an emergency a horse was kept saddled and bridled for each man—and a time or two when things looked very threatening we slept with the bridle reins over our arms. In an instant we could be in the saddle and gone. This was very unusual, but we were prepared and I am sure it avoided a stampede.

Night herding is an art in itself. A level bedding ground was selected and the herd held in as compact a mass as possible. There were always three or four old bovine hellions who insisted on sitting up all night and they never missed a trick. A strange noise or an unusual sight was very apt to set their legs in motion, and if badly frightened they would take the herd with them. Once a herd started to stampede they seemed to enjoy the sport and thereafter bolted upon every excuse. However, if an outfit was properly broke in at the beginning and carefully watched there was little danger of stampeding, unless from very unusual circumstances.

The night guards rode around the herd until they met, then they turned back and rode until they met at the opposite end. This was kept up until their two-hour watch was ended when the new men took up the same hand. During this time the waddies whistled or talked to themselves, sang songs or hummed, but whatever they did was in a low monotone. This was done to warn the cattle that they were near, and to avoid a prolonged quietness. The singing seemed to have a soothing effect on the cattle (but not on the other men). It also kept away prowling animals which might throw a scare into the stock—and it kept the riders from running unexpectedly into some critter who had taken a notion to drift away.

I wish I had written down the songs I have heard. Some were exceptionally good. The boys were in the habit of setting to rhyme stories of the trail, of gunfights, of cowboy heroes and of their sweethearts, which were sung on the night watches, and they were passed from waddy to waddy. We have many of the songs today, some of which are very popular [see "Cowboy Songs and Verses"]. They are as distinctive of that part of the American life—an epic which will never happen again—as are Stephen Foster's plantation songs.

I believe the finest singer I ever heard was Scorpion Pete, a scapegoat of a vagabond who we picked up later on the trail around the Boggy and was in more mischief, good and bad, than one can imagine. He was about the hardest customer I ever knew, but his long suit was good old church hymns, especially John Wesley's (the Methodist, not the badman) and he was soon known as the singing cowboy. I marveled at his memory. Hearing him at night, one would think they were listening to the tenor section of the Halleluiah Chorus. But let something disturb him or cross his path and he could curse an hour at a time and never double back on his trail.

Chapter Twenty-Three

Strays and Drags

Our average was but eight to twelve miles a day which was not helped at all when we ran into snow in the mountains of western Texas and blizzards on the plains of Indian Territory and Kansas. These storms were of short duration, but I think we suffered with the cold more than had it been winter.

The cows were already heavy with calf as we left the Brazos River and by the time we made the Red River crossing they were dropping from three to five a day. As it was impossible to trail the wee ones, and it had been proven impractical to provide wagons, it was necessary to kill them.

When we neared the occasional settlement farmers drove as far as fifty miles to meet the herds and pick up the calves. If we were lucky the Boss might trade a calf for some butter and eggs, a rare treat.

I have mentioned necking earlier. The longhorn mothers were noted fighters and they were right on the job to protect their young. They refused to leave their calves, so it was necessary to neck her to another cow in order to keep her in the herd. As soon as a rope dropped over her head things began to happen. As a rule she charged the first thing she saw, but once in a while she would pivot and go after the man who tossed the rope. It then became quite a scramble to get out of her way but at the same time tighten up the rope. The second man was always on hand to get his rope on too, and it wasn't long until she ended in a somersault and in a few minutes found herself yoked, or "necked," to another cow with a short length of rope.

If a cow managed to break back to her dead calf (or where it had been left) she stayed right there until the next herd came up. By that time she had discovered she could do nothing about it and was willing to trail along. It was customary for each herd to pick up the strays and drags and bring them with their own bunch. In 1871 it was a pretty sure thing we would never hear from our strays, although occasionally it did happen.

By 1878 the owners had worked out a scheme of procedure which was fairly well observed, if convenient. All cattle carried a road brand in addition to their own original brands. The trail boss had a bill of sale with the brand records. At most important river crossings and at all stockyards and terminals there were "reps" and "trail cutters" who inspected the brands, checked them with the bill of sale, and cut back all cattle not accounted for, which included the usual strays and drags picked up. They were then held or sold for the rightful owner. We picked up several drags which we dropped at Dodge where a rep of a preceding outfit was on hand to gather up his brand.

Hoof wear caused considerable trouble. The hoof would wear down to the heart, where grass and mud would lodge and the feet became so sore the critters could not travel. We had to leave them to shift for themselves, with the hope they would find their way into another herd and ultimately be paid for. When one had no rep to watch his interests, the critter was always sold and sometimes we got our money, but more often we didn't. The gals on the row got most of it.

Chapter Twenty-Four

Storms, Cyclones, and a Most Eerie Sight

A crew of fifteen or twenty men get along reasonably well on a cattle ranch where everything has melted down to a system which runs with the least possible friction. Even then nerves get jumpy and things happen. When the boss sees things are pulling up to a high tension he will shift the men to new duties or send them off to where they could reduce pressure by attempting to stand a town on its ear.

On the other hand, there is no chance for diversion while on the Old Cow Trail. Anytime there is diversion it is very apt to be trouble. Storms or unexpected excitement might start a stampede. Cool weather meant boggy trails, trouble at the streams, and hard work pulling cattle out of the mud. Rains mean twashy feet and loss of weight. Dry weather brings dust, insects, sweat, and sores.

Everyone was covered with the trail dust and alkali clouds that drifted along with the herd. Even when bandanas were pulled up over our faces the acrid dust sifted through and burned raw our noses and throats. Lips became so dry and cracked it was hardly possible to smoke and as one fellow said: "When I try to spit it goes up in steam and scalds my nose."

Every spot which was chafed in riding became either a sore, or what was worse, a callous. Fleas, skeeters, gnats, and flies all conspired to make life one merry round of irritation. Fights started over the merest trivial and some of them were settled with bullets after reaching the cowtowns. The men were too loyal to their boss to indulge their hatreds while on the trail.

I do not know anything which brought more genuine comfort and solace than a good chaw of tobakker—a quarter pound in one's warbag was equivalent to being a millionaire, and more comforting. It held down a gnawing tummy while you were hours away from food and one forgot about thirst when thoughts of it would drive a person delirious. It helped to soothe cracked lips and cut the alkali dust from one's throat. Then too there was a lot of fun using a chaw to practice one's marksmanship on the stinkbugs as they rolled manure balls along the trail.

However, I have painted the worst picture. In general we were very fortunate. We missed the worst storms and there were no dangerously swollen streams to ford. When too bad, the Boss held up the procession and we went into camp.

We never had a stampede, thank God in all languages. The fact is, it was considered very much against the credit of a trail boss to have a stampede charged against him. We did have one experience I shall never forget, and it verged on disaster but our good luck held.

We approached the North Canadian in murky weather. Night fell early and was decidedly black with signs of severe electrical disturbances. Heavy lightning lighted up the distant skies all night, and there was a continual roar. We had two experiences that night I shall never forget.

Before the storm broke, off in the southwest we could hear a distant rumble. We did not know whether it was a cyclone or a hailstorm, but either would have meant disaster as the herd was then ready to take off. The roar moved toward us and passed high overhead in the darkness, the whine and whistle causing a still vibration in our ears and it seemed to suck away our breath in a sort of vacuum. In a few moments all was dead quiet and then the rain set in. Our share of the storm was a heavy, steady shower. It kept us in the saddle all night, wet and miserable. God, how dismal and cold!

Then after night and rain had totally swamped us, electricity began playing on the horns of the cattle and along their backs while little fire-balls called fox-fire jumped across the ears of my horse.[1] It was a most eerie sight and rather spine-chilling as a glow took over the entire herd of 2600 cattle, with the heavy blackness of night as a background.

The cattle were as skittish as a prisoner before a judge and they milled restlessly. All it needed was just one "Boo" to take the lid off and make one hell of a mess of cattle, mud, and cowpokes. Every man was on the job as we expected the herd to hi-tail it most any minute, but as the hours passed we held the herd and come morning we had drifted but a couple of miles from camp.

A day or two later we overtook an outfit whose cattle had been scattered from hell to breakfast. They were then gathering up the odds and ends. They had been caught in the corner of a cyclone, the one which had passed over us, and it not only scattered their herd but demolished the chuck-wagon.[2]

For several days afterwards we had to sleep in our boots and let them dry overnight on our feet. To have taken them off would have resulted in hard, shrunken leather and an impossible job to pull on come morning.

Chapter Twenty-Five

Chef Par Excellence

Under such conditions the cook proved himself a jewel. He made life livable for us. It was true he was not the cleanest person living, but neither were we. A gang of cowpokes can not look like a lily and smell like a rose after weeks of trail life. I never knew his name, but he went by the moniker of "Joe"—and sometimes Pee Dee. He was known as Prairie Dog Joseph because he bragged he could cook Prairie-puppies to a king's taste, but who wants to be a king? We suspicioned he put some in the chuck anyway. However, it tasted alright and we figured it best not to ask questions. Instead of calling him Prairie Dog Joe, which would have put him on the warpath, we shortened it to P.D. and Pee Dee.

Joe was a real cook and he was well worth his pay of $100.00 a month which was as much as the Boss drew. A good cook can do more to keep life pleasant on the trail than all the rest combined. It made no difference how cold the weather, how wet, what the hour, we could always depend on Joe and his kettle of black coffee—what a lifesaver.

And that was only half the story. Joe would come sloushing thru the storm to see that every mother's son of us was served—and he always did a little kidding that cheered us. Joe kept a kit of skunk oil and badger grease for saddle sores and cracked lips, and rattlesnake oil for bruises and sprains. We conveniently forgot about the diamondbacks and skunk fat rendered in the kettle. There was a store of sage to brew in case of fever chills and he had picked up from the Indians a goodly knowledge about roots and herbs which he would administer regardless of the hour.

Most of the pokes were too proud to ask for such remedies. They preferred to play hero and suffer, but I am telling you they were mighty pleased when Pee Dee came slipping in on the quiet to offer a potion—and to the devil with the taste!

The bad water at the Salt Fork affected all of us but we wished to appear tough and would not admit feeling bad. I think we would willingly have sacrificed our last pair of breeches for the courage to ask Joe for "something, anything that would help." I had a bad time and at last decided I would wait until night, then snook over to the chuck-wagon to get assistance. As I neared the wagon I ran into one of the boys. Both of us were taken by surprise.

I said, "What in the Sam Hill are you doing here?"

He replied, "Oh, just tending to a call of nature."

I answered, "Well, the chuck-wagon is a fine place to be doing that. Why didn't you go the other direction?"

And he said "Well what the hell are you doing here?" We stood there a moment, then both of us had to laugh.

"Oh hell," he said, "let's wake up the cook and see what the old ruffian can do for us."

We did, but never told anyone about it.

Chapter Twenty-Six

Scorpion Pete and the Polecat

Down below Camp Supply on Wolf Creek, just before hitting the Boggy, and God what a boghole, was where we first picked up one of the oddest characters I ever met. Claimed he was whelped by a wolf, looked it, and said his name was Scorpion Pete, all set to use his stingers. We did not argue.

Polecats were very numerous along one stretch of the trail. It was rather hard to avoid getting on intimate terms with them, they being so friendly like. But we got through without social contact.

Naturally, talk turned to skunks and their penchant for biting cowpokes asleep on the ground, which often caused hydrophobia. We spun some windies about rabies, with some of the stories being hairraisers and a bad thing to go to sleep on. Scorpion Pete took the chatter so seriously he really got the jitters and crawled up in the hooligan wagon and insisted on sleeping with Prairie Dog Joe. [1] It took the butcher knife's threatening swings to persuade Pete his place was on the ground with the rest of us.

One night we cooked up a whiz of an idea. A skunk had been killed and the scheme was to tie a rope to the kittie and drag it up to Pete after he fell asleep. This was done. Then one of the pokes mewed like a sick cat and at the same time gave him a dirty pinch then we dragged the skunk over his arm at which the sleeping beauty came to life very sudden like. The first thing he smelled and saw was the polecat, just as it was moving into the darkness (being pulled away by the rope). Poor old Pete plum exploded, left his bedding ground with a horrible howl, and disappeared into the moonlight. He figured he had been bitten and was positive he was already a victim of the dread disease. In fact, he was so sure of it he went to wallowing and groaning and moaning pitiful like. The rest of us steers nearly split our breeches laughing.

The disturbance brought out the cook and he too thought the boy was in a real fit and away he rushed to the chuck-wagon for a remedy.

Imagine our surprise when he immediately returned with a pint bottle of likker and proceeded to pour it down the throat of the suffering man. Pete was so astonished he sat straight up, grabbed the bottle, and had its contents well on the way down his gullet before Pee Dee could retrieve his treasure. The very same thought hit every one of us—where the devil had that bottle been secreted, and how had the cook kept it intact? One of the boys wanted it and decided right then to throw a fit but his efforts were so ridiculous even the frightened cook got wise and knew he had been victimized.

Thereafter followed several reports of tarantula bites, but that too failed to bring out the medicine. "Blisters"—so called because his nose was always peeling—came limping in one day and claimed he had been bitten by a rattler. The cook looked at Blisters' boots and the heavy cowhide chaps which slopped down over them and decided no rattler could go through all of that leather.

He went away cussing and mumbling to himself, but we did hear him say, "When I see your damned tongues turn black and pop outer your mouths, you so-an-so liars, then I will believe you. Maybe."

Search as we might for that bottle of Pee Dee's, no one ever discovered where he had it hid.

Chapter Twenty-Seven

Buffalo Biscuits and Sow Belly

In a treeless country most cooks became real artists in obtaining their fuel supply. They can get up a meal on a handful of wood or a few "buffalo biscuits." Consequently it was very unusual for most cooks to make an unnecessary fire and more unusual for them to get out on a stormy night to make coffee and keep it hot for the shivering pokes. We sure appreciated that ours did and tried to help Joe when possible. We kept the water barrels full and as we worked the trail we would pick up odd pieces of wood or sage roots, or we would forage along the creeks for kindling. This we tossed into the "cooney" or "kitty"—cowhide suspended under the wagon where the fuel was kept. This provided dry wood and was a treasure house in which we kept the bank balance healthy.

Speaking of buffalo biscuits makes me think of the settlers who in the later drive came to the bedding grounds asking for the "cow-chips." I have been told four hundred to five hundred pounds of fuel could be picked up after just one night's bedding from some two thousand cattle. I believe this was the dry weight. Of course the chips had to season, which took but a day or so under a hot sun.

Sourdough bread baked in a dutch oven was served three times a day (the bakery not being just around the corner). Several of the ovens were used, and they were covered with hot coals. We always had plenty of sowbelly (too much most of the time) and gravy made from the meat fryings, flour, and water.[1] Black coffee, gallons of it, without sugar or cream. It was considered effeminate to use cream with coffee—ugh, it came from a cow! We were served tinned fruit or tomatoes once a day, and believe me, canned tomatoes with a dash of salt is just about the finest dessert you ever ate. Try it sometime when your gullet is so thick with dust the saliva turns to mud.

As we were on the move all of the time, the cook had to toss up a meal in an hour and have us fed. Any time we got held up for high water or had to rest the cattle Prairie Dog would mix up a concoction of some sort, it didn't matter what it was called, but it was always good and tasted fine.

The Boss saw that there was some dried fruit, but it was a luxury we seldom enjoyed. Our daily allowance was set at a pound of flour and three-quarters of a pound of bacon along with the other essentials. Fresh beef was seldom used. There was no way to save the meat in hot weather. Twice we were approached by begging Indians and the Boss figured it cheaper to pay tribute by butchering than to take chances of having the herds stampeded. I believe that was the only times we had fresh beef.[2]

Chapter Twenty-Eight

Surprised by Indians

While I saw but a few buffalo on the Chisholm Trail in 1871, there had been plenty of evidence of the immense herds. We saw many outfits going out to hunt, or returning with hides. But seven years later on the Texas Trail it was a different story. Before we crossed the Red River we met an old buffalo hunter who had been as far west as the mountains and all over the country that usually pastured untold thousands, and he told us "Boys, the buffalo days are over. I have traveled a trip of country 75 miles wide and 150 miles long and saw but a few scattered herds."

God loves fools and women. God was good to us and we weren't women so you guess what that made us. At the Canadian River in the I.T. the Boss was warned the local Indians had left their reservations and were evidently out for trouble. As they were reported to be Northern Cheyennes we discounted the warning as we did not figure we would see any that far west.

The year before, in 1877, Dull Knife and his Northern Cheyennes had been sent to the Darlington reservation very much against their will.[1] Unhealthy conditions led to trouble, and the Indians kept leaving the reservation on raids that extended a great many miles. After repeated warnings Dull Knife fulfilled his threat, and just a short time after we passed that country they took to the warpath and left a crimson trail that has no equal in history, either for strategy in avoiding the troops, or in viciousness when they reached the Kansas settlements [see "The Dull Knife Raid"]. Our trail boss was not a man to entirely overlook a bet. He figured he had better start filling his hand right then, so we filled our six-shooters, two to a man, and each of us drew a belt of ammunition. In addition, the cook kept a couple of rifles in readiness—but even then we were caught napping.

Soon after leaving the Canadian we sighted a bunch of buffalo, not a very large bunch, but buffalo nevertheless. We decided on fresh meat and in the distance was another outfit bent on the same mission, so we figured to beat them to the draw. The Boss rode off in the supply wagon, and how he did lay on the whip. It was a comical sight to see the wagon bouncing along with plenty of daylight between him and the wagon seat. I followed on my horse while the men stayed with the herd. Even then the cattle became restless at the sound of the rattling wagon and it took good management to hold them steady.

The buffalo took fright and away they went in that awkward gait so characteristic of them. We did not get close enough to shoot effectively, although we did pump considerable lead in their direction. Then we got the scare of our lives. We were so intent upon the chase we paid no attention to the other hunters—and then all at once we discovered we had run into a bunch of Indians. Talk about feeling one's scalp creep. Mine sure did! For a split second we wondered what would be next—by that time we had wheeled and were headed for camp as fast as our nags would go. My first thought was, "The Boss won't make a very nice looking corpse with those whiskers and minus a scalp." For myself I was thinking no one will say when laid out in a box, "My doesn't he look natural!" I looked back over my shoulder to estimate how much longer I had upon this earth when I discovered the Indians were hi-tailing it in the opposite direction as fast as turpentined cats and evidently as badly frightened as we. Well, that was just fine.

Later, upon reaching the Cimarron we saw another small herd of bison. This time they were some distance up the stream quietly browsing along the valley. Needless to say we took a careful survey of our surroundings before launching the attack. Assured there were no lurking savages, the Boss and I took in after the humpbacks. We did considerable shooting as we raced along, but my shots went wild. However, the Boss called his shots and killed one buffalo. This bunch of five or six were the last wild ones I ever saw.

Chapter Twenty-Nine

Two Bucks for the Orphans

The first cattle to reach Abilene was those of C. O. Wheeler who broke the trail in 1867 and the following year some thirty-five thousand were penned there. The ante was doubled the next year and by the time of my visit in 1871 something over six hundred thousand cattle came north over the trail. That was the peak year, and the last year Abilene enjoyed the distinction of being the cowboy metropolis of the world. Homesteaders had fenced away much of the grazing land, the country was settling up, and the people of Abilene decided they did not want any more of the notoriety they had earned the past four years when the city was known as the world's worst, a wide open brothel hell-bent-for-election.

That winter, or sometime early in 1872, three-fourths of the people of that country signed a petition, which was circulated over Texas, requesting the Texas cattlemen to ship elsewhere. The railroad had built on west, and Newton some sixty-five miles south was glad to grab the cattle business. However, it became noted more for its lawlessness than the cattle business done.

I am told the people of Abilene immediately recognized their loss and made every effort possible to rectify it by sending delegations and circulars over the cattle country, inviting the herds to come back, but the damage was done beyond recovery. It was not the petitions so much as the homesteaders. There was no longer sufficient forage, and there was always trouble with the settlers, so the trail jumped to Dodge City. It was my good luck to have been in Abilene at its "best" and seven years later to be at Dodge while she ruled the cowboy world, or rather, while the cowboys ruled Dodge City.

Fort Dodge was an important military post on the old Santa Fe Trail. With the coming of the railroad a new town was started on the north bank of the Arkansas, some five miles west of the Fort. The city itself was not much to get enthused over, but the volume of business conducted made one dizzy.

Dodge was a city divided against itself. The railroad, which ran east and west, was the dividing line—and the dead line.

North of the tracks, running parallel with them, was Front Street, which was several blocks long, with a plaza at one end. The principal block faced this plaza and this block contained the better class of business establishments, saloons, and dance halls included. Wright and Beverly's was the most important outfitting store. There were several barber shops, a post office, an opera house, the Iowa Hotel, the Wright House, the Dodge House conducted by Deason Cox, and Delmonico's.

Scattered along Front and its intersectioning streets were many eating joints, some twenty to thirty saloons, a dozen or more dance halls and gambling holes. Many of the establishments contained all three—saloon, gambling tables and dancing—and the girls who entertained at these places sold their favors along with the drinks they served. Then too the better residences were in this part of the city. The primary cross-street was Bridge, which led out across the Arkansas River toll-bridge. I do not wish to forget to mention the church. Yes, they had a church north of the tracks and a goodly attendance on Sunday. And let this thought sink in: When those waddies went to services they listened to the preacher and when the collection box was passed they went into their pockets and dug out a silver dollar while the pious brother snooked in a nickel and then went to sleep.

I mentioned Scorpion Pete, the singing vagabond cowboy who was so good with the Wesleyan hymns. Well, he suggested we go to church. He had been out on the town and had tried to drink her dry, but had not yet succeeded. He said, "By God, Charley, us Christians has got to stand together. Let's go up to the church and help them sing and pray."[1] I had no doubt about his ability to sing, but I did have serious misgivings about the prayer side of his life.

Pete led out the singing and slipped in an "Amen" in the proper spot. He was a very devout listener to the services and when we left he borrowed two dollars from me, thanked the parson for the pleasant and spiritually profitable evening, and handed him the two bucks "for the Orphans." He never did repay me and I am yet wondering who it was that counts as having paid the preacher.

Chapter Thirty

Chorus Gals

There was a street in Dodge City similar to Front, which also faced the tracks on the south side, and along its length was a string of cheap hotels, eating houses, dance halls, honky-tonks, can-cans, and what-have-you. Also there was the one story "jug" constructed of 2 x 6 planks nailed flat. On the roof of the jail was a one-room shack which housed the city dads. That was the first penthouse that I know of. Most of the corrals and livery stables were to be found in this section. There were just about as many buildings here and perhaps as many people, but those who lived on this side of the tracks were not at all particular about their morals.

The town here was wide open and anything went. Her proud boast was that her denizens always rode—either out of town on horseback or in the spring wagon to Boot Hill. While across the dead line (the railroad tracks) those good people attempted to run a law-abiding community along with their saloons, brothels, and dives—and they succeeded in doing so in a most commendable manner (that is most of the time). Their boast, too, was that the waddies rode both ways, either horseback as free men, or as whipped curs with their tails between their legs after being buffaloed and fined. One thing they insisted on—and enforced regardless of cost—all guns had to be registered as soon as one reached town. More than one man tried to argue, only to end with a busted jaw.

> A little powder and a little paint,
> Makes the chorus girl what she ain't.

There was usually a show or two going on in Dodge. They had an opera house and Eddie Foy ran the season. Several of us spent a dollar and a half each to see a performance. Afterwards an old codger who had been seated near the stage remarked, "Be-dad! Did you see that parcel of gals? And warn't they the wild fillys? Red stockings on, and danged if they didn't show their knees! Yes sir! More than their knees—from whar I was sittin, I seen more than their knees." I wonder what the old buzzard would say if he was to walk down our street today and seen some of these fat gals stuffed into a pair of gym pants.

Next day at dinner a couple of the girls came in. I have been wondering ever since what made them look so nice on the stage and so washed out when the fresh air hit them. Perhaps a little powder and a little paint did what the carpenter said: "It will cover over most any kind of a botched up job."

Chapter Thirty-One
Earp, Masterson, and Holliday

When the city dads in Dodge decided to father a law-abiding community, they followed the lesson of Abilene. They called on men who could shoot quicker and hit more accurately than the outlaws. After several miserable failures they brought in Wyatt Earp. It did not take him long to dehorn, brand, and trail break the would-be shootsters. He could talk to an enraged outlaw and was fast enough to buffalo them. Fact is he was perhaps the only man alive who could successfully accomplish it. Come fall and the last of the cattle drives of 1877 he went to Deadwood where things went high, wide, and handsome all winter.

Ed Masterson, who was city marshal while Wyatt was gone, tried to talk first and shoot afterwards and was downed by a couple of gunmen. Ed was killed April 9, 1878, and soon after that Earp was called back to take charge of things and to herd the pokes and buffalo hunters along the straight way and through the narrow gate. They intended to keep a church in town, and they did.

§

I was leaning against the wall of the Long Branch when an old buffalo hunter came in the door. He had all of his arsenal decked about his person, and the likker he had consumed had him pie-eyed and bow-legged. He went to the bar, pulled a six-gun, and said he was going to shoot out the lights, paint the town red, and throw the marshal out on his ear. Earp sauntered in and told him to hand over the shooting gear as everything had to be registered. The request was refused and further threats were made. At the same time he went for his other Colt with evident intention of following through his threats. Earp pulled an uppercut out of his hip-pocket, as the saying goes, and cracked the buffalo killer square on the jaw.

When the fellow picked himself off the floor he was as tame as a pet coon. The marshal received two to three dollars per arrest, and a percentage of the fines assessed. He told the hunter the jail was full, but for him to show up at the office and stand trial. This he did.

For the fastest dealing, and the prettiest hand-play, Doc Holliday stood tops. At this particular time Doc was in a run of luck and it didn't make any difference whether he stacked against chips or men, he always won on the draw. Later Doc became quite a pal of Earp's and saved his life in Dodge at a time when it looked certain both men would be killed. I don't know much about that story. However, Doc came to Dodge on the rush. It was reported he killed Ed Bailey at Fort Griffin and had been arrested. Friends of the deceased were getting likkered up for a necktie party when Doc's lady friend, Big Nose Kate, decided to take a hand before it was too late. She set fire to the rear of the hotel. As soon as she hollered "Fire!" every mother's son joined the fire brigade and rushed for the town pump. That was exactly what she expected. While the menfolk were so occupied she secured Doc's guns and a couple of horses, then went to the hotel room where he was held prisoner. A gun stuck in the ribs of the lone guard brought the desired results. They escaped to Dodge City and were there at the same time we were.

Chapter Thirty-Two
Bullets in the Air

Bob Wright, the man who started Dodge City, was its leading citizen as well as a state legislator. He had a very strong cowboy element in back of him, as well as the southside denizens. Opposing Wright, Mayor Kelly backed up Earp. Hard feelings ran strong between the rival factions. While I never heard of any shooting on their own part it was rumored Wright's faction had offered a thousand dollar reward for the Earp scalp. Several attempts were made to collect.

The air was full of stories. Some were for the law and many were agin it. The Texas bunch was hot and heavy against Earp and they kept sending up men who were known fighters whom they figured would down him. He either buffaloed them or set them up on Boot Hill where some one hundred fellow Texans now push up the lilies, put there by one man or another. Some of the toughs that went after Earp instead elected to turn tail and run as did Clay Allison, but death was preferable.

The Driskells and the King crowd were buddies and they hit Dodge at the same time. This was a year or so before I was there. After getting likkered up they decided it was time to hurrah the city and old Tobe Driskell undertook to do it according to the latest style. Tobe came down the street roaring like a wild Injun while his friends watched from their hangout. Earp stepped out to meet him. Tobe told Earp what his intentions were and he told it loud enough so every person within blocks could hear it. But before Tobe knew what really happened Earp had bent his .45 Colt's barrel over his head and proceeded to propel him to jail with a firm hold about his neck and breeches.

That night a large crowd of Tobe's henchmen secured a sledgehammer and undertook to batter down the jail door. They were nonplused when Earp faced the crowd and demanded they scatter. Earp thereupon centered his attention on two of the ringleaders and they knew they would be sacrificed if shooting was to start. Consequently they turned tail and hit for Arkansas.

§

While I was at Dodge, Wyatt Earp was shot at by a cowboy who rode down the street. Earp returned the fire. The following news item I have kept covers the story, although it is very much different than what was told on the street—

Bullets In The Air

Yesterday morning about 3 o'clock this peaceful suburban city was thrown into unusual excitement, and the turmoil was all caused by a rantankerous cowboy who started the mischief by a too free use of his little revolver.

In Dodge City, after dark, the report of a revolver generally means business and is an indication that somebody is on the warpath, therefore when the noise of the shooting and the yells of excited voices rang out on the midnight breeze, the sleeping community awoke from their slumbers, listened to the click of the revolvers, wondered who was shot this time, and then went to sleep again. But in the morning they dreaded to hear the result of the war, lest it should be a story of bloodshed and carnage, or of death to some familiar friend. But in this instance there was an abundance of noise and smoke, with no very terrible results.

It seems that three or four herders were paying their respects to the city and its institutions, and as is usually their custom, remained until about 3 o'clock this morning, when they prepared to return to camp. They buckled on their revolvers, which they are not allowed to wear around town and mounted their horses, when all at once one of them conceived the idea that to finish the nights revel and give the natives due warning of his departure, he must do some shooting, and forthwith commenced to bang away, one of the bullets whizzing into a dance hall near by causing no little commotion among the participants in the "Dreamy Waltz" and quadrille.

Policeman Earp and Masterson made a raid on the shootist who gave them two or three volleys, but unfortunately without effect. The policemen returned the first and followed the herders with the intention of arresting them. The firing had then become general and some rooster who did not exactly understand the situation, perched himself in a window of the dance hall and indulged in a promiscuous shoot all by himself. The herders rode across the bridge, followed by the officers. A few yards from the bridge one of the herders fell from his horse from weakness caused by a wound in the arm which he had received during the fracas. The other herder made good his escape. The wounded man was promptly cared for and his wound, which proved to be a bad one, was dressed by Doctor McCarty. His name is George By [Hoy], and he is rather an intelligent looking young man.   ➥ Dodge City Times, July 27, 1878

Chapter Thirty-Three

Ballin' the Jack

After leaving Dodge we balled the jack without event.[1] We hear of the Dust Bowl, but you should have seen it in 1878. It was then a seemingly limitless prairie, with the grass knee high. As the wind blew the grass rippled and waved which made the prairie appear to move. It was very much like looking at our own wheat fields now as the ripening grain plays in the breezes.

At no time did we travel a well-defined trail, although there were evidences of many herds having passed and at some bottlenecks the tracks were deeply rutted. We forded the Sappa some southwest of Oberlin, Kansas. Dull Knife committed a big massacre here not long after we passed [see "The Dull Knife Raid"]. Next we crossed the Republican just below its confluence with the Frenchman. We did not see the town of Culbertson—perhaps it was hidden behind the hills. However, while camped in that vicinity "Angel Face Johnson" came out to the herd. Finest Sky Pilot in the West.[2]

As we proceeded on up the trail we immediately took to the higher ground east of the Frenchman and our trail boss kept us pushing northward. The Blackwood could be seen to the east but before long we lost it. This was practically a new trail. We would drift back to the Frenchman for water and then locate a bedding ground away from the river.

If I remember rightly it took three days between the Republican and the last water on the Stinking Water. We had to be very careful as we worked along that creek, as the bottom was muddy and very dangerous. However, the North Stinking Water had a safe bottom and the cattle were permitted to range up both sides of the valley to the trail crossing at its headwaters, where there was a large spring.

At that time there was a cattle ranch at the spring. It seems to me it was called the "30." A willow pole bridge crossed the creek. It was stretching the imagination to call it a bridge. A few willow poles were laid lengthwise across the bog and creek, then some lighter pieces were placed crosswise, all of them lying on the ground. However, it served the purpose. The chuck-wagon went across, bounding along in finestyle. We could hear the rattle of the pots and pans and the cook's yelling above the bawling of the cattle. Pee Dee Joe said it was the wildest ride he experienced on the entire journey. It was close to this place where Rowley was killed that fall by some of the Dull Knife warriors.[3]

This was the jump-off for Ogallala and the last water until we reached the Platte. As soon as we crossed to the west side we noted trails coming in from the south and assumed the main trail laid some northwest of us. This proved to be correct. The grass was badly trampled and the loose soil was blowing.

The dry jump between the Stinking Water and Ogallala took two days and was the longest dry drive on the entire trip. The problems began the second day. There was a strong wind from the west and the old cows would throw up their heads and "think" they smelled water, and away they would go in that direction, making a terrible racket with their bawling and the clatter of their horns and hoofs. It took a lot of hard work to fight them back to the main herd. By that time some old pelters would decide they smelled water toward the east, and away they would go.

That fool herd kept us fighting them all the way. I never understood why they imagined water was east and west of the trail, but they never tried to find water north—and the only water in that entire country was north. When we did get within smelling distance of the Platte there was no holding the thirsty herd. However, the Boss had anticipated this and he had us fan the herd out over a wide space of country so there would be little or no crowding at the river.

Chapter Thirty-Four
Ogallala

That which has been said about Abilene and Dodge City pretty well covers the story of Ogallala. She too had a street which faced the railroad tracks but this time most of the business was conducted south of the track. I do not know if there was much of the town to the north, but I think the homes were and perhaps some of the stores. It should be kept in mind there was no place for the cowboys to loaf except the pool halls, saloons, dance halls, and gambling joints, so I must be excused for knowing more of the rougher element and amusements of these towns than of the solid business concerns.

Come evening most of the townsmen were also found to be in these places, although being there did not necessarily mean a man was drinking or gambling. I did not see many drunks but I did see a great many people conducting their pleasure in a sensible manner. It was surprising the percent of business which was transacted in these places while the men soberly partook of refreshments or played cards. In other words, a person could find exactly what he was looking for, whether it be genial companionship or a fight—a pleasant evening or debauchery.

I recall with pleasure the way we looked forward to a square meal at the hotels. The Rooney House set a good table. [1] Perhaps we appreciated it the more after weeks of sourdough biscuits and sowbelly floating in gravy. There was a table reserved for the "Drummers"—

those white collared, lily-fingered gents with the huge sample trunks. An orange or an apple seemed the principal differences between their fifty-cent meal and the cowpokes' two-bitter on the checkered oil-cloth.

Our gang decided we were as good as they, and we moved in on a party of them. Perhaps they didn't like the smell of our saddles, but neither did we of their perfume (they smelled like a chorus gal)—anyway we declared openers and decided to play the game close to our belly. It wasn't but a few minutes until they threw down their hands and got up to walk out. Well, so much for them, "good riddance" I said, and Blisters gives it an Amen by letting his spoon slip, unintentional like, which showered the nice gent's white collar with prune juice. Hi-pockets nearly swallowed his table knife, which was loaded with mashed taters, when Blisters apologized.

We were in Ogallala just a night or two and then moved on, crossing the Platte nearly opposite from town and then moving eastward down the river. We did not follow the bottoms, but kept as far away as practical in an effort to avoid the scourge of mosquitoes. Even on the high ground where the wind blew strong the skeeters caused much suffering to both man and beast. We did not see a house between Ogallala and the town of North Platte with the exception of a couple of section houses along the railroad.

Our cattle were destined for the Lee Ranch, which was a wonderful layout on the North Loup [see "The Ranches of '78"].[2] This ranch was a ways above that owned by the Olives on the South Loup whose manager was Miller. Before reaching the Olive Ranch one of our horses strayed away and a lame cow had to be dropped. The horse was one that none of us cared to ride while on the trail. He had a nasty disposition, was not at all trustworthy, and always acted as though he had a cocklebur under his tail.

After we got the herd to the home ranch I was sent back to Olive's to pick up both the cow and horse. This man Miller was a very pleasant sort of a fellow and we struck up quite a friendship. He had ridden the horse and wished to purchase it. Later on Mr. Lee sold the horse to Miller and he passed it on to some ranchers up the river. They could not manage the brute and he quickly won quite a reputation for tossing men. He made all of them choke the horn and claw leather and it was not long until he was a real outlaw.

I left for Illinois in September 1878 and was in Omaha the night the Grand Central hotel burned. For lack of something better to do I decided to take a ride on one of those horse street cars. All at once we saw a huge billow of black smoke raising up into the sky and the driver of the street car said, "My God, the Central Hotel is afire." The hotel was a new affair and was reported to have been the largest between Chicago and San Francisco [see "The Grand Central Hotel Fire"].

A short time after my return home I read in the papers of the killing of Ketchum and Mitchell by I. P. Olive and his men. I was very much surprised to read that news as my impression of the outfit was that they were a very fine bunch of men [see "The Killing of Ketchum and Mitchell"].

Chapter Thirty-Five

The Fighting Parson's Son

I became acquainted with the Reverend Potter while in the Spring country although down there he was known as the "Fighting Parson." Perhaps I will tell more about him later. [1] Just now I am thinking of his son Jack, who was known as the most entertaining liar on earth. Jack was well educated for his time but enjoyed depicting himself as the ignorant cowpoke. I have not the least idea where I got this clipping, but it's a typical story, and one I enjoyed [see "More on the Fighting Parson's Son"]. It seems, according to Jack's story, he had been north with a string of cattle. After various experiences on the train he stopped in Denver a day or two. He went to the barbershop to be roached and trimmed, and was induced to take a bath.

Here are the words of the Reverend's son:

The colored porter turned on the water, tossed me a couple of towels. I commenced to undress hurriedly, fearing the tub would fill up. The water was within a few inches of the top when I plunged in, then I gave a yell like a Comanche Indian for the water was scalding hot. I came out of that tub on all fours, but when I landed on the marble floor it was so slick I slipped and fell over backwards. I scrambled around and finally got my footing by taking hold of a chair. I thought, Jack Potter you have been scalded after the fashion of a hog. I caught a lock of my hair to see if it would slip, at the same time fanning myself with my large Stetson hat. I then examined my toe nails as they had received a little more dipping than my hair, but found them in fairly good shape, a little black but still hanging on.

Chapter Thirty-Six
Sam Bass and the Train Robbery

My acquaintance with Joel Collins was brief. As mentioned before, we rode together on the Chisholm Trail in '71. Joel decided a cowpoke's life was too hard a way to make a living and tried his hand at the easier way, robbing the gold stages in the Black Hills. Later, he with five other kindred souls robbed the Union Pacific train at Big Springs, Nebraska, nine miles west of Ogallala. They secured about $60,000 in gold from the express car and $600 to $800 from the passengers. Joel Collins and Bill Heffridge were both killed by U.S. troops as they crossed the Kansas Pacific tracks near Buffalo Station, Kansas [see "Joel Collins"]. Something over $20,000 in gold was recovered, which had been tied up in their chaparejos and swung across the front of their saddles. Jack Davis and Sam Bass escaped to Denton County, Texas, with their share of the loot, where Sam lived a Robin Hood sort of life for about a year.

The robbery was committed September 16, 1877, just a few months previous to my last trip up the trail. As we traveled through Texas and the Territory we heard tales of his exploits as he robbed banks, stages, and trains, along with sundry brushes with peace officers. Upon our arrival at Dodge we heard that Sam Bass had been killed in a battle with officers in Texas on June 21.

The last of the Big Springs train robbers were Jim Berry and Nixon, who escaped to Missouri. There is a lively story concerning these men in which it is claimed they hid their loot on the Frenchman, near Champion. That may be possible, but the rest of the story is mere supposition. It was claimed one man was killed and the other taken prisoner and soon died of his wounds in the Nebraska penitentiary, but this is without foundation.

Very soon after the robbery, parts of the song "Sam Bass" were being sung on night herd. As he became more notable more verses were added to the cowboy song. I will give you but a part of the ballad—

> On the way back to Texas they robbed the U.P. train
> And they split up into couples all over again.
> Joel Collins and his partner were overtaken soon,
> With all their stolen money they had to meet their doom.
> Sam met his fate at Round Rock, June the twenty-first
> They pierced poor Sam with rifle balls and emptied his purse.
> Poor Sam he is a corpse and six feet under clay,
> And Jackson's in the bushes, trying to get away.
> Jim had used Sam's money and didn't want to pay,
> He thought his only chance was to give poor Sam away.
> He sold out Sam and Barnes and left their friends to mourn,
> Oh what a scorching Jim will get when Gabriel blows his horn.
> Oh what a scorching Jim will get when Gabriel blows his horn.
> Perhaps he's got to heaven, that none of us can say,
> But if I'm right in my surmise, he's gone the other way,
> Oh yes, if I'm right in my surmise, he's gone the other way.

No one knows the origin of "Sam Bass." Without doubt many men donated a verse or two, or corrected verses, and I have heard many versions of it [see "Cowboy Songs and Verses"].

Chapter Thirty-Seven

Homesteading

In later life my homestead was south of Naponee, Nebraska, just across the state line in Phillips County, Kansas [see introduction]. We bored a well with an auger and went down some thirty to forty feet to reach water. At the thirty-three-feet level the auger struck something hard and we were unable to go further. At first we thought it must be a rock and had just about decided to call it a dry hole when we tried dropping the auger to see if we could break through the obstruction. After dropping it several times we felt the obstruction yield. A buffalo tooth was brought up that time and the next load brought part of a buffalo jawbone and another tooth.

Several other pieces of bone were then brought up. This cleared away the obstruction and we then went down some six or eight feet to a strong flow of water. The location was somewhat up a draw in the Republican Valley. It all goes to prove that the Republican River has shifted in ages past, and that there had been tremendous influences at work on that old river bed else those bones could not have been buried so deeply.

There was a very pious old Circuit Rider who had homesteaded near Bloomington, Nebraska, in the early days. We called him Brother Kennedy. At that time preachers yet smoked tobacco, some chewed, and some took liquor. The church was trying to discourage those bad habits and some of the preachers were living up to the new standards. He was one.

About 1873 the buffalo were yet quite plentiful southwest of Naponee. On a Sunday some of the townsmen would drive out and kill two or three and return Monday with the meat, which they peddled. Brother Kennedy asked if he could go with them, but he made it very plain he would do no hunting on the Sabbath. "I will go along in the wagon and see the hunt, but I will not kill any of the buffalo." Of course the men were delighted to have him go as he was well liked and made wonderful company when camping out. It would have suited them much more had he done some shooting, but as it was against his creed they respected his attitude.

It was then early fall and the buffalo were just beginning to bunch up preparatory to their migration to the high flats of western Nebraska and eastern Colorado where the winds would keep the grass blown clean of snow. The hunters returned Monday afternoon. One of the townsmen asked Brother Kennedy, "Brother, did you see any buffaloes?" and he replied, "My yes, praise God, I did. Yes I saw 10,000 acres of them."

Chapter Thirty-Eight

Trail's End, 1940

Time comes when we ride the range from the old kitchen rocking chair. It's hard, because we know it's the end of the trail. Once we damned the hardships that made aching bones, forgetting that come morning all pains had been caressed away whilst we slept against the warm bosom of Mother Nature, and each sunrise brought a new day and another opportunity. Oh well!—

Life is like a trip over the Old Cow Trail. We humans are all herded along helpless like, rattling hoofs, knocking horns and bellowing— and most of us want to be pointed along the trail. There's ever some hellions in every town ready to stampede at the first rumor—and some always wants to snook away from the bedding grounds to do a little prowling secret like.

Then there's the drags that must be hazed along and some as has to be necked to keep them manageable. But at the big end of the string are the old steadies and come hell or high water they hold to the trail. They know the faults of the world and don't give a damn.

The whole human herd is trail-driven to the river Jordan and the weak sisters and the spineless brethren has got to be tailed out of the mud; they always find quicksand to stand on. God loves them all, but danged if I know why.

The other side of the Jordan is the winter range, the great pasture whence no pilgrims return. There the sunset promises rest, but eternal rest buried in the cold bosom of Mother Nature.

Yes! We have the promise of a better day and a range where all callouses and trail sores are no more. I am planning on going to that Home Range some day, but just now I ain't the least bit homesick.

I have a hankering to catch up my war-horse once more and I want to fork an apple-horn saddle. I yearn to feel the sting from clouds of alkali dust and the sweet solace that comes from a chaw of tobakker. Food don't taste good any more, but I know I'd relish sitting on my hunkers at the tail end of the chuck-wagon, spearing sowbelly floating on gravy. Just once again I crave a can of steaming Arbuckle coffee and a sourdough bisket smeared with sorghum while off in the distance I hear the nightwatch singing to the herd—waiting for the break of dawn.

But I guess it's all wishful wishing. It's the age-old rebellion against Time and Tide. Ride the Trail Of Life each day but don't ask for tomorrow—tomorrow is the end of the trail.

⊗ ⊗

Charley Hester passed away at age eighty-seven in 1940 shortly after this memoir was completed. His obituary lauded him as being one of the last of the riders of the old Chisholm Trail.

Notes

1. Restless Spirit, 1869

1. The route of travel was via Clinton (see chapter 2). By the time a census enumerator came across them on August 22, Charley Hester—Charles Albert Hester—and the "Golden" party had made their way to Prairie City Township in Bates County. A sixteen-year-old C. A. Hester, born in Illinois, is shown working as a laborer and residing right next to a Charles *Golahon*. The data does not specify whether the places of abode were tents, wagons, or houses. See U.S. Bureau of the Census, *Ninth U.S. Census, Prairie City Township, Bates County, Missouri* (1870).

3. Southdown Country

1. This route parallels present-day U.S. Highway 69 through Oklahoma.

2. Hester almost certainly was referring to the Grand River (a.k.a. the Neosho River).

6. The Chisholm Trail

1. Nebraska City does not seem to have been the original destination. See "The Abilene Cattle Market Crash," this volume. Regarding the name of Charley's employer, court records concerning this drive reveal it was Ware, which was a pseudonym for W. H. Lockridge of the firm Lockridge & Geyers. See "Ware/Lockridge," this volume.

2. To illustrate the potential profit margins to be made herding cattle north at the time Charley was working the Southdown, the average per-head price in February 1871 was $7.37 in Texas, $28.84 in Kansas, and as high as $51.91 back east. *Report of the Commissioner of Agriculture for the Year 1870* (Washington DC: Government Printing Office, 1871), 47.

3. For a discussion by Hester regarding the specific route of the Chisholm Trail, see "Geography of Two Trails Traveled," this volume. Roughly, it followed the course of present-day Interstate 35 from Austin to Fort Worth, and U.S. 81 through Oklahoma.

4. Charley would have just recently turned eighteen.

9. Cowboy, Cowpoke, Cowpuncher

1. For a further discussion of the terms "cowpoke," "cowpuncher," "brush-popper," and "waddy," see Ramon F. Adams, *Cowboy Lingo* (Boston: Houghton Mifflin, 1936), 21–23, 158.

The word "waddy" was originally used to describe a rustler but evolved to mean "cowboy," especially a cowboy who was nomadic. Although generally accepted as being of unknown origin, it has been speculated the term was related to the ranchers' hiring of temporary help to "wad out" the regular crew during roundup. See Peter Watts, *A Dictionary of the Old West* (New York: Promontory, 1977), 357.

10. Six Inches to Hell

1. The prominent Illinois cattle broker Joseph McCoy founded Abilene in 1867. He built the first stockyards there and started the trail drive boom to Kansas after spreading word around Texas that the town was open for business. Joseph G. McCoy, *Historic Sketches of the Cattle Trade* (Kansas City MO: Ramsey, Millett & Hudson, 1874), 39–62.

11. The Murder of Marshal Smith

1. McConnell and Miles offered to plead guilty to a charge of second-degree murder in exchange for life imprisonment but were turned down by the prosecutor, who wanted to hang them. After a trial in Manhattan, Kansas, both were convicted. McConnell was sentenced to twelve years and Miles to sixteen. *Abilene Chronicle*, March 23, 1871, 3.

12. Eyes Like Gimlets

1. Having arrived in town in the spring, the Ware/Lockridge crew remained until early autumn. The cattle market in Abilene crashed that season, and a large number of herders pastured their livestock, waiting in vain for it to improve. See "The Abilene Cattle Market Crash," this volume.

2. Hester confuses the Drover's Cottage with the nearby American House, both of which were undergoing renovations around the time he was there. See *Abilene Chronicle*, May 25, 1871, 3.

15. Wild Bill and the Tinhorn Gamblers

1. They seem to have been playing a dice game called bunko, a.k.a. 8-dice cloth (Bunko player Holli Clark to Kirby Ross, May 5, 2003).

16. Trouble in Nebraska

1. After shipping in Abilene came to a halt in 1871 because of adverse market conditions, a number of drovers eventually sought out "other sources of disposal" in an attempt to avert financial disaster. The alternative disposal choice for Ware/Lockridge appears to have been Nebraska City, Nebraska. See "The Abilene Cattle Market Crash," this volume.

2. Court records resulting from the day's events indicate the crossing was actually near where present-day Hubbell, Nebraska, now stands. See "The Prairie Fire," this volume. En route to the Peru bottoms and the Nebraska City flats, they would have then followed Rose Creek past the site of present-day Thompson.

3. According to court records, this occurred around 9 AM on October 8, 1871, in southeast Thayer County, Nebraska.

4. Local resident Hubbell Johnson filed a civil claim for forty-five tons of hay valued at $225 and a fence valued at $25. Philander Kellogg filed a claim for a hedge and timber valued at $50. Court records show both men reached a financial settlement with Ware/Lockridge. It was also reported that a Mr. Gage lost hay, while a Mr. Keiser lost hay and grain. Charley's own words about "some of the other fire bills" suggest there may have been other victims.

5. Based on the path and boundaries of the fire reported in the local press and in court records, the conflagration burned an arc across the prairie fifty miles long that consumed at least a quarter of a million acres. For more on the fire, the victims, and the trial, see "The Prairie Fire," this volume.

6. Pursuant to a court order, the sheriff seized the herd as well as personal assets of the trail crew. The warrant was issued October 11 and the trial held October 14. The property appears to have been released upon the acquittal of the crew and the prompt monetary settlement of civil claims.

7. For further perspective into the cause of Ware/Lockridge's financial loss, see "The Abilene Cattle Market Crash," this volume.

17. Back in Texas

1. Edward Everett Dale, author of numerous books on the American West, was the longtime head of the department of history at the University of Oklahoma in the first half of the twentieth century. The "light of civilization" passage appeared in a 1929 journal article. See "Cowboy Songs and Verses," this volume.

2. Elmer Hester was a major Nebraska cattle rancher and ultimately donated over 8,400 acres of land to charity. See the introduction to this volume for more on Elmer as well as Charley's twenty-seven-year ranching association with him.

3. John Nance Garner of Uvalde, Texas, served as vice president under Franklin Roosevelt from 1933 to 1941.

4. The reference in the original memoir was Spring "county," which was either a memory lapse or a misspelling. There is not nor has there ever been a county by that name in Texas. The area around Rio Frio, which was part of Bandera County at the time, is known to this day as the Country of Eleven Hundred Springs—that is, Spring country.

5. The town of Rio Frio should not be confused with Frio Town. In 1877–78 Hester spent time around both.

19. Mr. Hiler

1. William Stevenson Hiler ranched primarily in Frio and Uvalde Counties. See "Javeline Hogs and Rattlesnakes," this volume.

2. Although it appears to have taken some time to be generally accepted by ranchers, the Texas legislature passed a law prohibiting mavericking in 1866 (coinciding with the rise of the politically influential cattle barons, who had much to lose to smaller, encroaching "entrepreneurs").

3. "So he said, 'I am Abraham's servant. The Lord has greatly blessed my master, and he has become great; he has given him flocks and herds, silver and gold, menservants and maidservants, camels and asses.'" Genesis 24:34–35. "Kine" is an ancient term for cattle that is used throughout the Bible.

4. Richard King, a sea captain, settled in South Texas in the 1850s and became a cattleman. By the time of his death in 1885 he owned five hundred thousand acres. Under the management of his son-in-law the King Ranch

continued to expand until it covered over 1.1 million acres by the 1920s. See Tom Lea, *The King Ranch* (Boston: Little, Brown, 1957).

5. More likely the cause for amusement was the simple, crass brazenness that was exhibited—brazenness that probably involved great animation and a smile. Lending support to this theory is the well-established fact that Richard King took a very dim view toward mavericking, especially where his own cattle were concerned. So adamant was King that he retained hired guns to act against perpetrators of the practice.

Taken in this overall context, Hiler's use of his branding iron in the very presence of King probably was quite humorous to all parties concerned. The same act undertaken surreptitiously or in an environment of less congeniality might have proven hazardous to Hiler's health. A lengthy chapter is devoted to King's efforts to protect his cattle in Lea, *The King Ranch*, 261–95.

20. The Texas Trail

1. This would have been around the time of Charley's twenty-fifth birthday.

2. John Richard Lee, an Irish immigrant, was a merchant, freighter, Indian fighter, and entrepreneur prior to starting his ranch in northern Nebraska. Hester's reference to New York possibly pertains to Lee's financial backers. See "The Ranches of '78," this volume, for more on Lee and his ranch. Lee saved substantially by buying his stocker cattle in the Lone Star State instead of further north. In January 1878—the very time the herd was being gathered for him—the average per-head price was $10.30 in Texas and $21.30 in Nebraska. *Report of the Commissioner of Agriculture for the Year 1877* (Washington DC: Government Printing Office, 1878), 171.

3. For a discussion by Hester regarding the specific course of what he alternately called the West Texas Trail and the Texas Trail, see "Geography of Two Trails Traveled," this volume. This route had a variety of names but has commonly been referred to as the Western Trail from Texas to Dodge City, and the Texas Trail or Northern Trail from Dodge to Ogallala and points beyond. See Harry Sinclair Drago, *Great American Cattle Trails* (New York: Dodd, Mead, 1965), 50–51, 193–205, 235–36. Roughly, it followed present-day U.S. Highway 283 through Texas and Oklahoma and then angled off north-northwest at Dodge City.

4. A trail herd from the Woodward and Oge was just ahead of Hester and

the Lee herd (part of which was gathered on the Woodward and Oge Ranch). For an account of their coinciding experiences during the 1878 season, see "Huffmeyer's Experience," this volume.

22. Run Along Little Dogie, Run Along

1. Not to be confused with the word "calf" or "calves." It is derived from the Spanish *caballo*, meaning horse. "Caballada" (pronounced "cava-yaw-da") was an expression used to refer to the string of spare horses in the Old West, with "cavvy" and "cavvy yard" being cowboy corruptions of it. Other commonplace terms for this type of herd were "saddle band" and "remuda." See Adams, *Cowboy Lingo*, 80; and Watts, *A Dictionary of the Old West*, 80.

24. Storms, Cyclones, and a Most Eerie Sight

1. Foxfire is also known as St. Elmo's Fire. See Watts, *A Dictionary of the Old West*, 320.

2. The Woodward and Oge outfit that was a day or two ahead of the Lee crew had a weather-related stampede as well as an experience with foxfire. See "Huffmeyer's Experience," this volume.

26. Scorpion Pete and the Polecat

1. "Hooligan wagon" is another term for the supply wagon. See Adams, *Cowboy Lingo*, 25; and Watts, *A Dictionary of the Old West*, 171.

27. Buffalo Biscuits and Sow Belly

1. "Sowbelly" is slang for cured pork from the underside of a hog. See Watts, *A Dictionary of the Old West*, 310. This was meat, not the digestive organ.

2. Indians also solicited beef from the Woodward and Oge and were refused. See "Huffmeyer's Experience," this volume.

28. Surprised by Indians

1. Around thirty miles west of present-day Oklahoma City, the Darlington Reservation was on the North Canadian River just northeast of Fort Reno. Hester would have been three days' ride to the west of it.

29. Two Bucks for the Orphans

1. Charley was an avid singer of religious songs and had the voice to harmonize with Scorpion Pete's tenor. Said Hester's obituary sixty-two years later: "He especially loved the singing and many of his old friends still remember his bass voice as he joined in the sacred hymns which were his favorites." See "Obituary, Charles Albert Hester." In addition, Charley's singing abilities remain legend within the Hester family to this day (Arletta Roundtree; Hester family lore).

33. Ballin' the Jack

1. Ballin' the jack—going fast. See Ramon F. Adams, *Western Words: A Dictionary of the American West* (Norman: University of Oklahoma Press, 1968), 12.

2. A sky pilot is a preacher or an evangelist. No additional information has been located on Johnson.

3. George Rowley had a cow camp along the Frenchman near Wauneta Falls in Chase County, Nebraska. While in Ogallala he heard that Indians were raiding, and he was killed along Stinking Water Creek while rushing home to his family. *History of the State of Nebraska* (Chicago: Western Historical Company, 1882), 968; Albert Watkins, ed., *Collections of the Nebraska State Historical Society* 17 (Lincoln: Nebraska State Historical Society, 1913), 43.

34. Ogallala

1. The Ogallala House was owned by S. S. Gast and was managed by his son-in-law, Sam Rooney. Robert R. Mahnken, "Ogallala: Nebraska's Cowboy Capital," *Nebraska History* 28:2 (April 1947).

2. Located near present-day Brownlee, Nebraska.

35. The Fighting Parson's Son

1. Hester never got around to discussing Reverend Potter in his memoir, but a profile on him has been located and can be found at "The Fighting Parson," this volume.

The World
of Charley
Hester

Geography of Two Trails Traveled

•❖ Charley Hester (ca. 1939)

Both trails, the Chisholm and the Texas, had their inception in the tremendous reservoir of beef in southwest Texas. Naturally, all the cattle did not travel these trails. Texas was literally covered with them as the drivers took the most accessible and direct routes. As I have previously stated, certain influences developed the above trails, and sooner or later most of the drive entered one or the other, depending mostly upon the year traveled.

The West Texas Trail was not used to any extent until conditions closed the Chisholm. As there were no towns and the cattle centers were widely separated, it is impossible to say just exactly which I traveled. I do remember most of the creeks, certain peculiarities of the trail, and the river crossings. We have checked this with the volumes of the Texas, Oklahoma, and Kansas historical societies, as well as The Chisholm Trail by Rider,[1] and other sources of information. Mr. Sutton prepared a detail of many of the two trails, which was later compared to those in the Chronicles of Oklahoma, vol. XIV, March 1936, and we find they agree.[2] We have therefore accepted that the following itinerary is a composite of the two trails I traveled. Roughly speaking the map of the two trails can be pictured by the letter "Y." Both Trails used the lower portion, with the trails forking at Elm Creek in Wilson County.

The Chisholm: San Antonio, Texas; New Braunfels; San Marcos River; Austin River, two or three miles below Austin; Round Rock; Georgetown; Salado; Elizabethtown; Bolivar; St. Jo; Red River Station, Mouth Fleetwood; Head of Mud Creek; Monument Hill; Wild Horse Creek; Rush Springs; Washita at Lime Creek, Rock Crossing; Canadian near Fort Reno; Prairie Springs; Kingfisher Creek; Hackberry Creek; Shawnee Creek; Salt Fork; Pond Creek; Polecat Creek; Bluff Creek; Caldwell, Kansas; Cow Skin Creek, Arkansas River; Wichita, Chisholm Creek; Sandy; Smoky Hill; Abilene; Republican River; Nebraska line, Rose Creek near Thompson; Fairbury; Peru; Nebraska City flats.

The Texas: Coleman; Bell Plains; Baird; Albany; Fort Griffin; Double Mt. Forks; Doan's Store, Red River Crossing; North Fork Crossing east of Soldier's Peak; Gyp Springs; Elk Creek, straight south of Soldier Spring; Oak Creek; Washita River, at Custer's 1875 camp; Canadian River at a little creek; Persimmon Creek; Wolf Creek at Boggy, God knows it's bad; North Canadian at Clear Creek; Doby Springs; Cimarron River at Redoubt Creek, deep hole crossing; Kansas, Dodge City; Sappa, southwest of Oberlin; Republican at Frenchman; North Stinking Water at Springs; Ogallala, Platte.

≈ ≈

This selection is from the Hester memoir.

"Southdown Country"

Hester does not elaborate on his use of the phrase "Southdown Country." Bell County histories make no mention of a Southdown, and contemporary Bell County historians profess a lack of knowledge about it. There does exist a breed of sheep called Southdown, and Bell County has long been a relatively large producer of sheep in Texas going back to the 1870s. So abundant was the animal in the county that by 1880 their numbers actually exceeded those of range cattle.[1]

It is speculated the term "Southdown," perhaps a bit derisive, was either general cowboy jargon that meant sheep country or was an expression unique to the cowhands Hester worked with and/or to Hester himself.

The Abilene Cattle Market Crash

It is quite possible Ware/Lockridge (see "Ware/Lockridge") initially intended to sell his herd in Abilene as opposed to Nebraska City. According to town founder Joseph McCoy, the Abilene cattle market collapsed in 1871 after a record six hundred thousand head arrived in Kansas. With many herders declining to sell at the low prices being brought in the vastly oversupplied marketplace, thousands upon thousands of cattle were pastured on the plains for months on end.

Compounding the problem, the season was an unusually rainy one, with the prairie grass used as feed becoming "coarse, washy and spongy," said McCoy. Consequently, the longer the cattle were pastured the more they became "poorer in flesh instead of fatter," causing them to be worth even less in their underweight condition.

"A great number of the herds were held until fall, hoping the later markets would be better, but when fall came there was but little better demand," McCoy noted. "In consequence of the [large] number and poor condition of the cattle, the markets were over supplied and many shippers met disaster, and not a few financial ruin. Finally shipping had to be entirely abandoned, and other sources of disposal looked up."

Ware/Lockridge was one such cattleman who stayed over until fall. Eventually he seems to have come to the conclusion that such "other sources of disposal" might be found via the feedlots of Nebraska City, where his stock could be corn-fed to improve their poor weight prior to sale under more favorable supply and demand market conditions. While the plan might have been sound in theory, it depended wholly upon the cooperation of the cattle and failed miserably on that point. Adding insult to injury, sandwiched in between the disasters suffered in Abilene and Nebraska City was the calamity that took place outside of Fairbury, Nebraska.

It should be noted that Ware was not alone in his failure that year. Said McCoy of the 1871 season: "Many drovers lost more than their all; others, who previously regarded themselves as being worth seventy-five to one hundred thousand dollars, found themselves suddenly made bankrupt."[1]

Ware/Lockridge

Charley's employer during the 1871 drive is a bit of a mystery. He presented himself to the crew and others as "Ware" but also went by the name of W. H. Lockridge. There are many possible reasons why he may have done this, including having creditors, the law, or personal enemies after him.[1]

There was a "Wm. H. Lockridge" who became the foreman/range manager for the Cheyenne & Arapaho Cattle Company in 1883, with headquarters near the boundary of present-day Blaine and Custer Counties, Oklahoma. It was said of him: "Mr. Lockridge is a range man of experience and ability, and will, as heretofore, make a successful herd manager and general range man for his company."[2]

The Prairie Fire

The fire of the Ware/Lockridge trail crew occurred the second week of October 1871 and, by rough estimate, burned around four hundred square miles of land (256,000 acres). Through a strange coincidence it began on Sunday, October 8—the same day the Chicago Fire started as well as the Peshtigo Fire in Wisconsin, which was one of the worst natural disasters in terms of human toll in U.S. history.[1] At the time, both of these other Midwest fires served as a backdrop to reports of the Ware fire in the local Fairbury and Beatrice newspapers.

Fueled by extremely strong winds, the Nebraska blaze started near the present site of Hubbell, burned two dozen miles northeast, and passed to the west and north of Fairbury before jumping the Little Blue River below the hamlet of Bowerville.

From there it went in an easterly direction, continuing toward the Big Blue twenty-five miles away, traveling the entire width of Jefferson County and fanning out into Gage County to the east and Saline County to the north. Had the area been in a later stage of development rather than predominately unsettled prairie, the damage undoubtedly would have been much greater and probably would have included loss of human life.[2]

WINDY.

The wind bowled over the prairies of this section, last Sunday and Sunday night, at a rate frightful to behold and fearful to hear. It came from the south, and brought from that region a decided touch of warmth, which, however, lasted only until Monday morning, when it shifted to the north, toning down, at the same time, to quite a respectable little blow. The smoke arising from the burning prairies, mixed with clouds of dust, constituted a pillar of fire by night and a cloud by day, as constant, if not as comforting, as that by which the children of Israel were led up from out of Egypt.

➡ Beatrice Express, Saturday, October 14, 1871

Terrible Prairie Fires

Destructive prairie fires have been raging in all parts of the west, and Gage county has suffered, among others. The continued warm weather had so dried up the grass that a spark was all that was necessary to start a flame, which before the driving south winds of last week, was liable to become a terrible engine of destruction.   ➡ Beatrice Express, Saturday, October 14, 1871

Destructive Prairie Fires.

The high south wind of last Sunday night was sufficient to fan the slightest spark into a roaring, driving sheet of flame. Whether the fires which a day or two before have been burning close to town had traveled eastward, or whether they came from the Otoe Agency, the work of some careless Indian hand, is not known.　　　　　　　　➻ Beatrice Express, Saturday, October 14, 1871

On Monday afternoon and evening we observed a large fire burning in the vicinity of Bowerville. We learn since that it did considerable damage, burning some hay for Mr. Gage, and some hay and grain stacks for a Mr. Keiser who lives near Bowerville. The burnt district embraces a tract commencing about 5 miles north from here, extending to Swan Creek, and reaching nearly to Beatrice.

➻ Fairbury Gazette, Saturday, October 14, 1871

Quite a lively trial was had here last week on the arrest of some drovers who had in charge some Texas cattle. While camped on Rose Creek the prairie took fire as a result of their carelessness and considerable damage resulted. Whether they were guilty of criminal negligence in allowing the fire to escape, we don't know, but if a few of these Texan drivers were fined occasionally for their acts of lawlessness we think such accidents would be less frequent.

➻ Fairbury Gazette, Saturday, October 21, 1871

Cowboy Songs and Verses

In chapter 22, Charley laments that he wishes he had written down the songs he heard on the trail. Around the turn of the twentieth century, historians started compiling some of these old word-of-mouth, unpublished songs into books, including The Life and Adventures of the American Cow-boy (1897) by Clark Stanley, Songs of the Cowboys (1908) by N. Howard Thorp, Cowboy Songs and Other Frontier Ballads (1910) by John A. Lomax (who is perhaps the most respected chronicler of these cowboy songs), The Song Companion of a Lone Star Cowboy (1919) by Charles A. Siringo, and American Ballads and Songs (1922) by Louise Pound. Forewords and other notes in these books discuss the origins of the songs and generally reflect Charley's own statement about their having been passed orally from cowboy to cowboy.

The "Sam Bass" song in chapter 36 is found in all of the above-referenced publications, and the "cow by the tail" song in chapter 6 appears in most. While Charley may not have known the latter one to have a title, it came to be known as "The Old Chisholm Trail" and is one of the most recognizable trail songs today.

In 1919 John A. Lomax published *Songs of the Cattle Trail and Cow Camp*, which was described at the time as being "a by-product" of his aforementioned 1910 *Cowboy Songs and Other Frontier Ballads*. In the introduction to his later book Lomax noted he was unable to identify the original writer for a large number of the compositions he documented. He further stated that this particular project was the result of "what seemed to me to be the best of the songs created and sung as [the cowboys] went about their work."

Contained in the later book was a work by an author Lomax was unable to identify entitled "When You're Throwed"—which turns out to be the "when a fellers been a straddle" piece that Charley relates in chapter 10. Like Lomax, Charley also specifically referred to it as being a "song."

Five years after Lomax published "When You're Throwed," a cowboy bard by the name of Bruce Kiskaddon put out a book of poetry entitled *Rhymes of the Ranges*, in which a different version of the words appeared. Since then, the words have commonly been credited to Kiskaddon and have been republished many times over the years as a poem. Regarding authorship, according to archivist Steve Green of the Western Folklife Center in Elko, Nevada, "When You're Throwed" is widely accepted as a twentieth-century Kiskaddon composition.

While no secondary documentation has been located pertaining to the sod/God "old cowboy song" in chapter 17, Edward Everett Dale's "light of civilization" phrase quoted by Charley came from a June 1929 article published in *The West Texas Historical Year Book* entitled "The Romance of the Range." The full passage relating to it states as follows:

Ranching has existed in the United States as a frontier pursuit since very early times. Almost [all of] the first English settlers along the Atlantic seaboard brought cattle with them, and as the better lands along the coast were taken up and planted to crops, men owning a considerable number of animals removed farther west in order to find pasture for their herds on the unoccupied lands of the wilderness. Thus once agricultural settlement was well started in its westward march across the continent, there was to be found along its outer edge a comparatively narrow rim or border of pastoral life. For a century and more it was there, slowly advancing as the area of cultivated lands advanced, a kind of twilight zone with the light of civilization behind it and the darkness of savagery before. The ranchmen could not push too far out into the wilderness because of the fierce tribes of Indians that inhabited it. On the other hand they could not linger too long on their original ranges or they would find themselves crowded and hemmed in by the men who depended upon cultivated crops for a livelihood. The American people had become "that great land animal." They pushed eagerly westward, occupied lands formerly devoted to grazing, cleared fields and planted crops, thus forcing the livestock growers again, and again to move on to "new pastures." (emphasis added)

John Wesley Hardin

The opportunities were several, in both time and place, for Charley Hester to have crossed paths with John Wesley Hardin between March 1870, when Hester started for Texas from western Missouri, and the spring of 1871, when he moved north from Austin with the Ware/Lockridge trail herd.

Born May 26, 1853, Hardin was just four months younger than Charley. In the process of putting his reputation "under construction" Hardin killed his first man at the tender age of fifteen in late 1868. In the course of the next two years the young killer was to dispatch at least another one dozen men, and many more thereafter in the years that followed his acquaintance with Hester.

In the summer of 1870—around the time Charley hired on in the Southdown country of Bell County—Hardin is known to have traveled from Navarro County to Round Rock, Texas. The most direct route would have taken him directly through Bell County. Four months later, after killing victim number eight, Hardin was captured as he fled to Mexico. While transporting their charge to Waco, the posse traveled into Bell County. After passing through the county seat of Belton, the party made camp. In the quiet of the night, the guard on watch dozed off. Taking advantage of the lapse, Hardin murdered all three members of his escort as they slept.

From there the fugitive again headed for the border and on the way stopped off at the home of his aunt, Martha Hardin Clements. While there his first cousins James, Mannen, Joseph, and Gip Clements talked him into joining them on a cattle drive to Kansas, where he felt he would be safe from arrest. With the name "John Wesley Hardin" becoming widely celebrated as a result of his series of killings, the outlaw assumed the name Wesley Clements for the next few months and assimilated into the Clements trail crew.

On the journey north, it did not take long for him to start making a reputation under the new name. By the time he had passed through the Indian Territory, two Native Americans had lost their lives—one on the Canadian River and the other near the Kansas state line.

Then, on the Little Arkansas River above Wichita, the herd immediately behind the Clements started pressing too closely. An altercation ensued and six Mexican drovers lost their lives—five by the hand of Hardin/Clements.

Word traveled quickly, and by the time he reached Abilene around June 1, "Wesley Clements," having killed a total of seven men on the cow trail, was a local legend. Even Wild Bill Hickok, who is quoted as referring to the man as "Little Arkansas," seemed to do his best to steer clear of trouble with the newcomer according to the accounts.

During his stay in Kansas, Hardin quickly enhanced his reputation in the aftermath of the July 5 murder of Billy Cohron (a.k.a. Coran), a popular and respected twenty-two-year-old "boss herder" from Bell County, Texas. With Cohron's brother John and Hugh Anderson, also from Bell County, Hardin/Clements tracked down the assassin and killed him with a bullet to the forehead in a saloon near the I.T. border.

Hardin returned to Abilene and almost a month later perpetrated the hotel incident that Charley recounts in his memoir. On the night of August 6, 1871, Charles Couger was shot in his room at the American House. Hardin, later writing of the incident, admitted he committed the killing there—supposedly to protect himself—after which he jumped from the second floor, stole a horse, raced out of town, and four days later set out for Texas.

As stated by Charley, Hardin ultimately was captured on a train in 1877. Hardin arrived at the Travis County Jail in Austin in August 1877—generally coinciding with Hester's second stay in the Lone Star State. After a trial the next month in Comanche, Texas, Hardin was returned to Austin and was incarcerated there until September 1878, when he was moved to the state penitentiary in Huntsville.

While Charley confused the site of Couger's murder, such a mistake is understandable given the passage of decades. Just as significantly, a similarity exists between the hotel in which the killing actually occurred and the one Charley mistakenly recalled it as occurring in: the Drover's Cottage Hotel had undertaken a major renovation in the spring of 1871, while the American House was reopened under a new name and new ownership around the same time after having been closed for "refitting" (see chapter 12, note 2).

Hester also claimed that Hardin was referred to as "Arkansas" in Abilene that summer. Hardin himself chronicled being referred to as "Little Arkansas" in his personal memoir. Some writers, perplexed by the nickname, state that its use has never been explained. Given that John Wesley Hardin's fame (or, more precisely, Wesley Clements's fame) in Abilene was directly tied to his killings of five Mexicans on the Little Arkansas River south of Abilene, the origin of the moniker seems to be quite clear.

Furthermore, Charley Hester stated, "I had heard of Arkansas being known as John Wesley Hardin, although it was not generally known." A newspaper report that was published in the aftermath of the hotel shooting verifies Hester's claim that the locals were unaware of Hardin's true identity:

The most fiendish murder was perpetrated at the American House, in this place, on the night of the 6th inst. The murdered man's name was Charles Couger, and that of the murderer Wesley Clements, alias "Arkansas."

➤ Abilene Chronicle, *August 10, 1871*

The article goes on to assert: "Coroner J. M. Shepard held an inquest on the body of the deceased, and the jury rendered a verdict to the effect that Charles Couger came to his death from a bullet fired from a pistol by Wesley Clements. No cause for the murder is yet known."

With the passing of a week, there was still no indication Wesley Clements's true identity was known:

To make this item more interesting, the man who killed Charles Couger on the 6th inst., in this place, also shot and instantly killed the Mexican who killed young Cohron. ➤ Abilene Chronicle, *August 17, 1871*

Had it been widely known that Arkansas, a.k.a. Wesley Clements, was John Wesley Hardin, it seems likely the newspaper would have reported it. And even if the newspaper reporters were so incompetent that they were not able to ascertain that which was common knowledge, neither did the coroner or his jury—a jury that would have been drawn from the same general population that supposedly knew the "truth."[1]

Charley Hester also claimed Hardin's motive for the killing was to silence a man that knew Arkansas' true identity. While this particular "cracker or cake" (see the introduction to this volume) claim is likely to meet with more debate than any other in Hester's memoir, there is evidence supporting it. According to the *Topeka Daily Commonwealth* of August 9, "A man was shot in Abilene last Saturday night. Two men in disguise entered his room, at the American House, and fired two shots into his breast. The assassins escaped and had not been reported captured at last accounts. They are supposed to have been former partners of the murdered man." This same article claimed the motive might have been due to a "pecuniary" dispute but also made it clear this aspect was mere speculation.

There were no known arrest warrants issued for John Wesley Hardin or Wesley Clements or Arkansas in Kansas prior to the American House murder, even in the wake of his string of killings of cowboys in the state. Conversely, there clearly were warrants out at the time for John Wesley Hardin in Texas. Had Charles Couger been previously acquainted with Hardin as asserted by both Hester and the *Topeka Daily Commonwealth*, then a longstanding mystery of motive for the killing may have been made a bit more transparent by the memoir of Charley Hester. This hypothesis is further bolstered by the body of evidence showing that the general public of Abilene was generally ignorant of the fact that Hardin and Arkansas were one and the same man, giving Hardin a motive to try to keep it that way.

In a postscript to the hotel shooting affair, one final closely related controversy arises. It has long been claimed in certain quarters that John Wesley Hardin once killed a man because his snoring disturbed Hardin's sleep. Whether this actually occurred is open to conjecture, but some historians have, without scholarly support, seized upon the lack of known motive for the killing at the American House in Abilene and have deduced that the snoring murder must have occurred there.

Cracker or cake, Charley Hester's account sheds light on the legend and myth of John Wesley Hardin and in the process draws into further doubt the snoring story—at least as far as it pertains to Charles Couger and the hotel in which he was slain.[2]

The Death of Hickok

Although Hester was back on the cow trail headed for Nebraska when Hickok shot Abilene saloon keeper Phillip Coe, he certainly would have heard various stories about it over the months and years that followed. Because of his strong personal dislike of Hickok he appears to have chosen to accept one that cast Hickok in an unfavorable light.

Many theories arose regarding why Jack McCall murdered Hickok in Deadwood several years after the killing of Coe. McCall himself initially said he had done it to avenge the demise of his brother at Hickok's hand but subsequently claimed a man named John Varnes had hired him to commit the assassination. While it is unknown whether Varnes or McCall had been friends of Phil Coe, the basic substance of McCall's latter explanation has the air of truth to it since it was definitely against his own self-interest to make such a claim. He was hanged afterward. [1]

The Ranches of '78

During the 1878 season, Charley Hester trailed cattle up from Texas to stock a new ranch in north-central Nebraska for John R. Lee, an early pioneer of the region. Lee was born in Ireland in 1839 and immigrated to the United States with his father and two siblings in 1850. After the arrival of the rest of the Lee family the following year, they farmed for a time in Pennsylvania before moving to Wisconsin in 1854 and then on to Dodge County, Nebraska Territory, three years later. [1]

As he became an adult, John Lee worked as a buffalo hunter on the plains of western Nebraska. By the time he was twenty he was running a trading post on the Pawnee Indian Reservation and became fluent in that tribe's language. After participating in several battles during a war between the Pawnee and the Ponca, he drove freight wagons across Nebraska from Fremont to Fort Kearny. During the mid-1860s

Lee was a subcontractor for the Union Pacific as the transcontinental railroad was built through the region. In 1869 he founded Wahoo, Nebraska, built the first home there, and operated the post office, store, and blacksmith shop. While living there he also opened Saunders County's first settler ferry across the Platte. By 1877 the frontier beckoned, and he moved to the Black Hills, where he operated a hay run between Deadwood, Dakota Territory, and Laramie, Wyoming, and fought in a war between the Pawnee and the Sioux.[2]

At this time the grasslands of north-central Nebraska had yet to be settled by the ever-pressing tide of farmers but did have a few cattle operations scattered across the area. Taking advantage of the free rangeland, in the late 1870s Lee started one such enterprise on the North Loup near what is now Brownlee in Cherry County (it appears Charley Hester was part of the crew that brought up the first cattle to stock this ranch). An absentee owner, Lee hired a man named Banks to run the ranch the first years of its existence.[3] The "wonderful layout" that Hester mentioned was likely a reflection of what John R. Lee's descendant Ava Lee Roseberry once described as "lots of grass in the wet meadows and plenty of water and few homesteads."[4] Furthermore, the ranch was surrounded by a series of natural lakes.[5]

By the time he was forty years old, in addition to the North Loup ranch Lee owned over 1,000 acres of land in Saunders County, 620 acres in Douglas and Dodge Counties, and 100 lots in Wahoo. But without his direct oversight, the cattle operation languished as winter losses mounted due to the failure of the foreman to put up hay for feed. To better manage the business Lee moved there and took charge of it. Drawing upon his prior experience as a merchant, he soon built a store that doubled as a restaurant and inn for the oncoming deluge of settlers, and in the process he organized the town of Brownlee in 1886.[6]

While most other open-range ranches in the area had to cease operations once the homesteaders made their way into the area, the entrepreneurial Lee adapted by having others file tree claims on parcels of government land, for which Lee planted and tended the saplings himself (up to thirty-five thousand per year). When the requisite time period had passed and the original straw men assumed ownership of the property, title was then passed on to Lee for a nominal payment.[7] In due course he gained control "of nearly seven thousand acres, which is one of the most extensive ranches in Cherry county, nearly all of it good hay land and stocked with a large herd of cattle and horses."[8]

While living in Cherry County Lee also ran a haying operation, sold farm implements, and served as Brownlee's first school director, justice of the peace, and postmaster. As he reached his final years in the early twentieth century he moved to Washington State, where he passed away in 1914.[9]

§

Before Charley Hester trailed cattle into Nebraska for Lee in 1878, one of Charley's employers during his second sojourn in Texas was the NOX outfit, located above Rio Frio in what is now Real County (a portion of which was originally part of Bandera County). *The Trail Drivers of Texas* places the NOX Ranch "seventy miles west of San Antonio, on the Frio River, thirty-five miles north of Uvalde."[10]

Hester also spent some time working in Frio and Uvalde counties, gathering the herd for John R. Lee from the Woodward and Oge Ranch and the Hiler Ranch (for a Hiler profile, see chapter 19 and "Javeline Hogs and Rattlesnakes"). Louis Oge and the Woodward family were South Texas institutions who made significant contributions to the history of the state. John G. Woodward moved from Mississippi to Texas in the 1840s, where he took up ranching on the Medina River southwest of San Antonio. Accompanying Woodward on this migration were his wife, Mary Ann, and sons, Montcalen, born 1841, and Caven, born 1843.[11]

In 1847 a fifteen-year-old immigrant from Goersdorf, France, Louis Oge (pronounced *O-zhay*), came to live with the Woodwards. Three years later Oge left the Woodward Ranch, joined the Texas Rangers, and saw duty with the legendary Big Foot Wallace on the frontier between San Antonio and the Rio Grande. From 1852 to 1856 a stage line that made the mail run between San Antonio and El Paso employed Oge. It was in this job that he first made a name for himself when, in August 1854, he led a convoy of seven wagons and thirteen men past a cordon of hostile Indians after a sharp skirmish.[12]

Following a stint from 1856 through 1860 working for Butterfield & Company carrying mail between Tucson and Fort Yuma, Arizona, Oge served in the 33rd Texas Cavalry (CSA) during the Civil War and rose to the rank of first lieutenant. Upon his release from a Federal prisoner-of-war camp in 1865, he went to Frio County and engaged in the cattle business.[13]

As Oge was making his way in life, so too were the Woodward boys. Coming of age in the 1860s Mont also joined the 33rd Texas Cavalry, where he served under Oge. After the war both he and his brother, Caven, took up ranching on the Leona River southeast of Uvalde and then were married—Caven to Julia Newton, and Mont to Helena Thomas, a first cousin of Sam Houston. As Cav's family grew, he moved over to Frio County in 1870 and joined Louis Oge, who was now his brother-in-law after marrying Julia's sister, Elizabeth.[14]

Mont remained on the Leona ranch and managed its growth until it grew to around forty thousand acres. In partnership with Ben Slaughter, another major rancher in the region, he regularly trailed cattle into Kansas. According to *Frio County, Texas: A History*, so prominent was Mont in the business that Woodward, Oklahoma, came to be named for him (a claim that might be disputed by Woodward County historians).[15]

Meanwhile, Caven Woodward and Louis Oge formed their own partnership in 1873 and established a ranch of at least forty sections (25,600 acres) on the west bank of the Frio River four or five miles above Frio Town. Shortly before Charley Hester's arrival four years later, the Woodward and Oge Ranch was the site of the last Indian raid in Frio County. Led by Oge, who was captain of the government-armed home guard militia, the ranch crew, a number of men from Frio Town, neighbor William S. Hiler, and a company of Texas Rangers took up pursuit of the raiding party and recovered fifty stolen horses.[16]

After moving many herds north in the course of a decade-long association, Oge sold his share of the ranch to Cav in 1882 and moved to San Antonio. A year later Woodward's health began to deteriorate, and he followed his old friend and partner into the city. Shortly after moving into a home next door to Oge, Woodward died at just forty years old.[17]

Woodward's widow afterward returned to Frio County. Oge remained in San Antonio, engaged in the profession of money lending, was elected city alderman, and served on the school board. In 1906, at age seventy-four, he was naturalized as a U.S. citizen, after which he lived another nine years before passing away in 1915. Mont Woodward was not so fortunate and, like his brother before him, met a premature death. While moving to Cochise County, Arizona, in the early twentieth century, he intended to start another ranch in that area but was robbed and murdered instead.[18]

Javeline Hogs and Rattlesnakes

William Stevenson Hiler migrated from Claiborne Parish, Louisiana, to Bexar County in the Lone Star State shortly after the birth of his second child in November 1853. By 1857 he was living on the frontier southwest of San Antonio with his family, now grown to three children, and made his home in that area until his death almost four decades later. In putting down his roots Hiler began ranching in far southeast Uvalde County on the Sabinal River near its confluence with the Frio, just a few miles upstream from the Woodward and Oge (see "The Ranches of '78"). He ultimately acquired additional land and cattle holdings in Frio and Guadalupe Counties.[1]

After being sidetracked for a couple of years serving the Confederacy in the 36th Texas Cavalry (CSA) during the Civil War, Mr. Hiler expanded his operation, initially with the help of his two oldest sons, James Banister Hiler and William Napoleon Hiler.[2] Writing of this period before he died in 1947, Joshua Lee Hiler, William S. Hiler's last surviving son, told of an Indian raid on the Hiler Ranch that occurred when he was seven years old:

When we lived on the Sabinal about 1871, a bunch of five Indians came by the house one day and were seen by my brother Wesley who was driving two horses toward the house. He had passed between the Indians and the house before they saw him. He took his horses to the house and told my father that he saw the Indians pass as though they were going to come into the road a short distance below the house. My father took the boy's horse and ran down the road to where they were just coming into it. He shot at them two or three times, he said, and they kept going and paid very little attention to him. He came back to the house and he and my two older brothers ran down the road, overtaking the Indians about a mile below the house. They were ready for fight and had joined about twenty more who were still on foot. Of course, the fight didn't last long. No one was hurt. The Indians came on down to the next ranch where they had a fight; then they came about two miles farther where they found a good bunch of horses, all of which they took with them.[3]

Despite being formed in 1858, Frio County was not organized until 1871 and until then remained under the governing jurisdiction of Bexar County. When it finally was organized, Hiler bought lots in Frio Town, the new county seat, and moved his family there—possibly to take them out of harm's way in response to the recent raid.[4]

The outlying ranch operation continued, prompting old cowboy John Henry Thompson to reminisce in 1939 about his time on the Hiler spread three years after the Indian scare and three years before Charley Hester met the cattleman (this also serves to illustrate the conditions of the range that Charley later worked):

I went to Frio County and went to work on the Hiler Ranch. Hiler told me I would have to have my leggings, jacket and leather elbows down there. That was in '74 that I went there and I tell you, there were acres and acres of solid prickly pear higher than a man on a horse and you couldn't ride through lots of it. It was a regular home for them old javeline hogs and rattlesnakes. I've seen some of the biggest old snakes come out of there I ever saw in my life . . . .

[Hiler] worked five or six men as a rule and there was Jim and Bill Hiler besides. I worked there that winter and helped gather cattle in the spring to take to San Angelo. They wanted me to go up with them to San Angelo, but I quit 'em up the road. . . . Guess it was a good thing I didn't go on with them for they got into trouble with some sheep men up there and Jim got shot in the hip. He got well but he was always crippled. The cattlemen and sheep men were always having trouble.[5]

Notably, at this time William S. Hiler had a second job—as sheriff of Frio County. Whether by coincidence or design, he resigned that position around the time of the San Angelo gunfight.[6]

During this period he also served as school trustee and senior warden at the Frio Lodge. Then in March 1877—several months before Hester met him—Hiler assumed the position of county judge. Finally, after living in Frio County for seven years, in 1878 Hiler moved his family to Uvalde.[7]

Over the years the prominent Southwest Texas pioneer had a total of eleven children. Mr. Hiler suffered his share of family tragedy, beginning with the death of his son Jefferson Davis Hiler, at age four, in 1865. Eight years later, seventeen-year-old Wesley, who had survived the brush with Indians in 1871, met his own untimely end as he succumbed to the hazards of ranch life and was killed by a horse.[8]

When grown, the remaining Hiler children and their issue spread throughout the American Southwest and could be found carrying on the family ranching tradition in the Texas counties of Uvalde, Frio, Medina, Presidio, Sterling, Jeff Davis, and Tom Green; on into Sierra, Dona Ana, and Grant counties, New Mexico; and as far west as Cochise County in Arizona.[9]

In his final years, William Stevenson Hiler—the man Charley Hester simply but respectfully referred to as "Mr. Hiler" and lauded as having "worked hard and rode far"—retired to Frio Town and finally back to Uvalde, where he died in 1893 at age sixty-five.[10]

Huffmeyer's Experience

Adolph Huffmeyer, nephew of Louis Oge, wrote an account of an 1878 cattle drive over the Western Trail that directly relates to Charley Hester's memoir for several reasons.[1] First, Hester mentions the Woodward and Oge and made a passing reference to having worked there during the winter of 1877–78. Hester and Huffmeyer were very possibly acquainted with each other. Furthermore, Hester spoke of heading north in "early March" while Huffmeyer's crew left "the first of March." Both departed from the same vicinity and went to Ogallala, Nebraska. En route, both herds were held up at the Red River crossing by high waters and then bogged down in quicksand in that waterway when they finally forded it.

In addition, Hester and Huffmeyer spoke of seeing lightning play across the ears of their horses and of being caught in a severe storm. Finally, both outfits had Indians solicit beef from them and both engaged in somewhat amateurish chases of buffalo herds. Given the close proximity of the two trail crews, it is possible they were dealing with the same buffalo herd and same Indians.

Here is Huffmeyer's account (written in 1920) of his experience on the cow trail in 1878:

The next year, 1878, we gathered our herd early and were ready to start by the first of March. This herd was taken through by Virgil Johnson, who died several years ago.[2] We had about two thousand head of mixed cows and steers. It happened to be a wet season and we lost a great deal of sleep from the very start until we reached Red River, on account of the excessive rains. At Red River Station we found about a dozen herds scattered over the country waiting for the raise in Red River to run down so they could cross that stream.[3] While we were here a severe thunderstorm came up and rain fell in torrents. While it was in progress I could see the lightning playing on the brim of my hat and the tips of my horse's ears. Suddenly a terrific bolt of lightning struck right in our midst and killed nine of our best cattle. It stunned my horse and he fell to the ground, but was up in an instant and ready to go. The cattle stampeded and scattered and it was all that we could do to keep ahead of them. After running them for a mile or more, every man found that he had a bunch of his own to look after, they were so badly scattered and frightened. I managed to hold 236 head the balance of the night, and when daylight came we worked the bunches back together and made a count and found that we had lost over three hundred head, which meant some tall rustling for the boys. Before night we had rounded up all of the strays except about forty head, which we lost entirely. We waited a couple of days longer for the river to fall, but it seemed to keep rising, so Mr. Johnson decided to ferry our chuck wagon over and swim the herd across. When we struck the stream it was bank full, with a sandbar (quicksand) showing in the middle of the river. In order to get the cattle to take the water we brought our work oxen down and started them across. They seemed to know just what we wanted, for when they reached the edge of the water they walked right out into the deep current and began swimming across, the balance of the herd following. Four of our steers stopped on the bar of quicksand and bogged down and we had to swim out and extricate them after we had all the others on the far side. Every one of them showed fight when we pulled him out of the quicksand, and took right after us, and we had to hustle to keep out of reach. On the other side of the river we found the bottoms full of ripe wild plums and enjoyed quite a treat.

When we took the trail again we could see the Wichita Mountains in the distance, about seventy-five miles away. We knew the trail passed along the foot of those mountains, but on account of water the trail made a big curve to the right, which made it a longer drive, so in order to save time, Mr. Johnson decided to try to go straight through on a bee-line to the foot of the Wichitas, and thus save several days. It proved to be a bad venture for we traveled without water for two days, not a drop for the cattle to drink or with which to quench our thirst. We had to keep traveling, and by noon the third day our herd was strung out for fully two miles, with the big steers in the lead going like race horses, and the old dogies bringing up the rear. I happened to be on the point and about noon I saw the leaders throw up their heads and start to run. Mr. Johnson said, "They smell water," and, sure enough, after crossing a ridge we found a little stream of clear sweet water. We camped right there that day and all of the next to allow our stock to rest. The country was open and was covered with the finest grass I ever saw. We reached the Wichita Mountains and got back on the old trail. While traveling along we permitted our herd to scatter and graze, and as we were proceeding slowly we discovered a brown bunch of something on a ridge about a mile away. It turned out to be a herd of buffalo, which were the first I had ever seen. We decided to go forth and kill some of the animals and, accordingly, several of us mounted fresh horses and put out to go around them and head them toward our herd so the other boys could get a chance to kill some of them. But when within two hundred yards of the buffalo they saw us coming and struck a bee-line for the north pole. We yelled and fired at them without result, they kept on traveling. I gave out of ammunition and was determined not to go back empty-handed, so I took down my lariat and selected a young bull about two years old, and soon had him lassoed, but found out that I was not fooling with a two-year-old cow brute. I think I let that bull run over my rope a dozen times and threw him each time, but he would be up in an instant, and I just could not hold him. I called Shelby to my assistance, and the two of us finally managed to get him down and cut his throat. Shelby went back to the herd while I remained and skinned the buffalo and had him ready to load into the wagon when it came along. . . .

While we were in the Osage Nation an Indian chief and four bucks came to our camp one day and wanted us to give them a steer or two for allowing us to graze our cattle through their reservation. Mr. Johnson refused to give them any, and the Indians went away in an ugly humor, threatening to come back and stampede our herd that night and get one anyhow. Mr. Johnson told them to just try that trick and pointed to our Winchesters. Of course we expected trouble, but the Indians failed to carry out their threat. Everything went along smoothly after that. It rained on us frequently, but only showers. . . .

We reached Nebraska. . . . When we reached the Platte River we found protection for our herd in the draws or ravines there. We delivered the herd at Ogallala and my uncle, Mr. Oge, sold all of the cow ponies and outfits and all hands took the train for home. [4]

Custer and Hester

Charley Hester lived a major portion of his life, including his last days, near Parks and Benkelman in Dundy County, Nebraska (see the introduction). Locally, Custer is associated with a skirmish against Cheyenne and Sioux led by Pawnee Killer just south of what is now Benkelman at the Republican Forks on June 24, 1867, and another skirmish northwest of there shortly afterward. Within days of these encounters Lieutenant Kidder's patrol was overrun as he pressed toward Fort Wallace in western Kansas after failing in an attempt to rendezvous with Custer.

Custer is also associated with a U.S. Cavalry encampment at Roundhole a few miles south of Benkelman in Cheyenne County, Kansas. Combined with Charley's passing by Custer's Washita battleground site in the Indian Territory during the 1878 trail drive, these connections to Custer so close to Hester's home at the time this memoir was written apparently prompted his strong interest in Custer. [1]

The Dull Knife Raid

In the spring of 1877 the clan of Northern Cheyennes led by Old Chief Dull Knife surrendered to U.S. forces at Fort Robinson in the far northwestern corner of Nebraska. Within a few weeks these people—close to one thousand in all—were taken to the Darlington Agency near Fort Reno on the North Canadian River in the Indian Territory.

Accustomed to the cool, dry northern climate, the Cheyennes struggled in the more oppressive environment, and within two months two-thirds of them were sick. According to one prominent member of the tribe, Wild Hog, "very soon after our arrival there the children began to get sick and to die. Between the fall of 1877 and the fall of 1878 we lost fifty children by sickness."

In the summer of 1878 a group led by Little Wolf met with Indian agent John D. Miles and pleaded to be allowed to return to their homelands in Montana and the Dakotas. Upon being denied this request, Little Wolf advised Miles that his people would nonetheless be leaving and that, if Miles were inclined to try to stop them, to do it away from the agency so its ground would not be soiled with the blood of the dead.

On September 9, under the leadership of Dull Knife and Little Wolf, 89 men, 112 women, and 134 children moved north and within forty-eight hours were overtaken by a contingent of cavalry on the Little Medicine River. After fighting for several hours the soldiers withdrew, having lost three men and having wounded five Cheyennes.

As the Cheyennes moved into Kansas, from September 17 through September 23 three or four ranch hands were killed and over one hundred head of livestock were stolen. Hearing of the approach of the Dull Knife band, the alarmed citizenry of Dodge City organized 50 volunteers to join 147 troops of the 4th U.S. Cavalry out of Fort Dodge.

Once again the military leadership proved to be somewhat tenuous, and after a small fight the force under Captain Joseph Rendlebrock withdrew. Shadowing the rapidly moving Native American fugitives, two days later the Bluecoats spent the day lightly probing Dull Knife's defenses. Sensing the soldiers' hesitation, the Cheyennes moved en masse that night and Rendlebrock let them go.

The following morning Dull Knife came across a group of hide hunters just south of the Arkansas River. Upon receiving assurances of safety by Dull Knife, the white men surrendered without a fight and the Indians were able to obtain a large supply of rifles and ammunition.

After crossing the Arkansas a few miles west of Dodge City, it began to dawn on the leadership of the Cheyennes that they were doomed if they continued to be delayed. Thereafter, they hastened their journey and traveled north virtually nonstop for the next three weeks.[1]

As the Cheyennes entered the Sappa Creek watershed in northwestern Kansas, their mood changed markedly from one of self-defense to one of raged aggression. Some of this group had been living on the Middle Sappa three years previously when two brothers from the frontier town of Kirwin, Kansas, were buffalo hunting in the vicinity. As Joe Brown was taking a load of hides to Fort Wallace, a band of unidentified marauding Indians attacked the hunters' camp and killed his brother Daniel and another man.

Upon returning to find the dead men, Joe joined a number of other hunters in the area. Holding a parley in which an attack on Native Americans was discussed, the undermanned outfit thought better of it until they came into contact with a forty-man patrol of the 6th U.S. Cavalry, after which the two groups combined forces.

In the early morning hours of April 23, 1875, they found a group of Northern Cheyennes encamped in southern Rawlins County at a place called Sappa Hole, which by day's end would forever after be known as Cheyenne Hole. The ensuing battle, if it can properly be called that, was a resounding victory for the white forces, which suffered only three casualties—two soldiers killed, along with the vengeance-consumed Joe Brown, who intemperately charged forward with a revolver blazing in each fist only to meet his destiny at the hands of several butcher knife–wielding Indian women. At least twenty-seven Cheyennes—perhaps many more—met their deaths in the fighting. As the village was put to the torch, the Indian dead, including women and children, were tossed into the flames. In later years, the words "massacre" and "atrocity" would become attached to this affair.[2]

Later that spring some of those surviving Cheyennes made their way to their home grounds in the northern United States, and on to the group led by Dull Knife and Little Wolf—after which, through a twist of fate, they found themselves returned to Cheyenne Hole three years later.

At this sacred place in 1878 there was no controlling the Dull Knife warriors. What followed was the carnage along the Sappa that left a "crimson trail that has no equal in history," according to the overly dramatic hyperbole of Charley Hester. That which had only recently been grassy, unbroken prairie now consisted of grain fields and sod houses—symbols of loved ones gone and lifestyle lost that released a pent-up anger which raged unchecked for two days—the "viciousness when they reached the Kansas settlements" that Charley Hester spoke of sixty years later.

Like the innocent Cheyennes before them, in the first days of autumn 1878 so too did another group of innocents—men, women, and children—also lose their lives. By the time Dull Knife had passed through, forty settlers lay dead and the event became ingrained into the collective consciousness of the region forever. "The Last Indian Raid in Kansas Museum" in Oberlin memorializes the deaths, while the town cemetery a few blocks away—originally created to bury many of the dead—maintains a towering monument to their memory.[3]

§

With the warriors sweeping out on the flanks, the main body hardly slowed as the Cheyennes continued their homeward journey. Moving down the Stinking Water, George Rowley's rush to his family put him directly in the path of Dull Knife and he, too, lost his life, as later mentioned by Charley Hester.

As thousands of U.S. troops in the area sat curiously paralyzed, Dull Knife proceeded unhindered. By October 4 the Northern Cheyennes forded the South Platte and moved across the railroad just four miles west of Ogallala. From there they passed the North Platte and then split into two groups—one led by Little Wolf, who took nearly all of the warriors straight north; the other, mostly women and children, which followed Dull Knife and moved northwest toward Fort Robinson.

On October 23 Dull Knife surrendered his group to the 3rd Cavalry near the military base. Ten weeks later he was informed that his tribe's great journey was in vain and that they were to be returned back south to Fort Reno. On January 9, 1879, these desperate people again took flight under Dull Knife's leadership. With the soldiers in close pursuit, a bloody fight took place a few miles away and within twenty-four hours fifty Cheyennes lay dead and sixty-five more were once again in custody. Nine days later another thirty-two were surrounded eighteen miles from Fort Robinson. When the shooting was over there, only three women survived. Dull Knife persevered and moved on across country with his family, evaded capture, and made his way to the Pine Ridge Agency, where he lived out his life.

As the final, hopeless escape of their kinspeople was being suppressed in northwest Nebraska, Little Wolf was futilely trekking along the Little Powder River in southeast Montana, where he was also captured. While his group was allowed to stay north, the other bloodied remnant was taken back to the Darlington Agency in the Indian Territory. Subsequently immortalized by the book *Cheyenne Autumn* as well as the movie by the same name, the so-called Dull Knife Raid was thus brought to an end. [4]

The Grand Central Hotel Fire

The Grand Central Hotel, Omaha's first major lodging facility, was erected from 1871 through 1873. Occupying one-fourth of a block, the brick edifice stood four stories high. It was leased to Charles, James, and Richard Kitchen in the spring of 1878 after changing hands earlier that year owing to a foreclosure of bank and builder debts totaling over $200,000.

Hester's belief in 1878 that "the hotel was a new affair" was correct in a sense. Just three months before the fire, the hotel had been closed for extensive renovations, including the installation of an elevator. On the evening of September 24, 1878—five days before the hotel was to be reopened—furniture deliverymen discovered a fire in a newly constructed elevator shaft. Rumors later circulated that as the alarm was sounded and an announcement made throughout the city, one of the elevator installers jumped up from his supper at a nearby restaurant and exclaimed that he had left a candle burning in the elevator shaft.

In the course of fighting the blaze, five firemen entered the third floor with a hose. Shortly afterward the interior of the building collapsed, and the men were almost instantly consumed in a mass of flames. Efforts to extinguish the inferno were unsuccessful, and the hotel was a total loss.[1]

The Killing of Ketchum and Mitchell

Ishom Prentice "Print" Olive was one of Nebraska's most prominent citizens in the summer of 1878. Controlling a large amount of land at the confluence of Spring Creek and the South Loup River, Olive ran thousands of cattle on his Custer County empire.

Reputed to be generous and courteous to those with whom he was on good terms, he did not hesitate in using deadly force against anyone he perceived as an enemy. Olive was a native of Williamson County, Texas, where at an early date he had killed two men aligned against his family. After the death of his own brother in an escalating conflict related to that event, Olive—with his younger brother Bob, who had also killed two men—moved on to the safer surroundings of central Nebraska. While Print had been cleared in his Texas shootings, Bob was a wanted man. With a price on his head, the younger sibling was using the alias Bob Stevens.

Once in Nebraska it did not take the tempestuous Bob Olive/ Stevens long to become embroiled in a simmering feud with Ami Ketchum, who boarded with a farmer named Luther Mitchell at the eastern edge of Custer County. Cattle theft was a common problem in Olive's part of West. When rustler Manley Capel was caught in the act he allegedly implicated Ketchum as an accomplice in the enterprise. Seeing the opportunity to deal with his enemy, hotheaded Bob Olive was deputized by Sheriff David Anderson in adjoining Buffalo County and went to the Mitchell farm with three allies on November 27, 1878.

Attempting to surprise the two sodbusters, the Olive men galloped into the farmyard with guns drawn. Ketchum immediately drew his own Colt six-shooter, while Mitchell went for his Winchester. Afterward one of the four raiders was to claim that Ketchum came as near to being the devil at that moment as any man he ever saw. In the blaze of gunfire that ensued, Mitchell also pulled his share of duty in backing Ketchum against the invaders to his property.

When the smoke cleared three of the Olive men had been hit, with Bob taking a shot through the body. After lingering for three days at a nearby farmhouse, he died. Mitchell and Ketchum, realizing that the reaction from the powerful Print Olive wound be swift and severe, decided to seek refuge in Merrick County, where they had previously resided.

Hoping to rally aid from all quarters, Olive put out a $700 reward for the arrest of the fugitives. In the meantime Mitchell and Ketchum backtracked toward Custer County intending to turn themselves in. En route they stopped in Loup City and spoke with an attorney, who advised them that to proceed further would mean certain death. While the men remained in town for another day or two to decide their next move, the sheriffs of Merrick and Howard counties, seeking to claim the reward, assumed the initiative and arrested the fugitives.

Unwilling to turn their captives directly over to Olive, the lawmen transported them to Kearney. Olive reacted by making it clear that there would be no money paid unless the prisoners were handed over to him personally. In stepped the sheriffs of Howard, Buffalo, and Keith counties, all of whom appeared to be more than willing to transport the prisoners to Olive's avenging clutches in Custer County.

Sheriff Gillan of Keith County gained the advantage and hustled Ketchum and Mitchell onto the morning train December 10, 1878, with a destination of Plum Creek. In the process Gillan moved the prisoners out of the oversight of their attorneys, who had let it be known that they intended to travel with their clients so they could ensure that no harm would befall them. As the train was on its way, the lawyers telegraphed a station along the route and left word that they wanted Gillan to hold their clients at Plum Creek until they could arrive on the next train. The sheriff wired back and said he would comply with the request.

As the train pulled into the station at 3:00 that afternoon, Print Olive and several of his men were waiting at the depot. The captives were immediately loaded onto wagons and transported toward the Olive Ranch.

Traveling nonstop all afternoon and through the night, the party arrived at Devil's Gap, just across the South Loup from the Olive Ranch. At that point Sheriff Gillan took his leave and Mitchell and Ketchum were escorted over to an elm tree. With the men still hand-cuffed together, two ropes were thrown over a limb and then noosed around their necks. One account published not long afterward claim-ed that Olive thereupon alternated hoisting and lowering the men for brief intervals, after which he doused their clothing with coal oil and set them on fire. Ketchum—who was given credit for delivering the bullet that caused Bob Olive to linger in agony for three days—was finally pulled back up and as he danced in midair, still shackled to his comrade, Print Olive took a rifle and shot him. The rope on Mitchell was then pulled taut, and he assumed his place on the makeshift gallows beside Ketchum.

When found the next day, the bodies were burned beyond recogni-tion. Olive never took credit for that aspect of events, and it has been speculated in some quarters that the wadding from the rifle shot set the prairie grass on fire, or that two drunken Olive men later returned and torched the dangling bodies. In any event, word of the burnings— coupled with graphic photographs of the two very charred victims— outraged the populace of the state.

The judge of the judicial circuit, realizing Print Olive effectively owned the jury pool, the sheriff, and the county court judge of Custer County, chose to try Olive himself at the Adams County District Court in Hastings. Convicted after a widely publicized trial, Olive was sen-tenced to life imprisonment.[1]

The defense promptly appealed the matter to the Nebraska Su-preme Court, with the primary point being that the trial should have been held in the district court of the county in which the crime was committed. By a two-to-one vote the appellate justices agreed and ordered a new trial. Because of a legislative oversight, however, when Custer County had recently been created it had not been assigned to a judicial district and the matter passed on to the county court by default. As the trial judge had feared, the die was cast. Little time passed before the following entry regarding Print Olive was written in the Custer County court account book: "The court finding no complaint on county docket and no complaining witnesses, the court orders that the prisoners be discharged till further proceedings can be had."[2]

The "further proceedings" never transpired, and Ishom Prentice Olive immediately moved on to greener pastures in Kansas and then Colorado, where he was gunned down in Trail City six years later.[3]

The Fighting Parson

•➤ John Warren Hunter (1920)

No name was more familiarly known thirty-five years ago in West Texas than that of Andrew Jackson Potter, the "Fighting Parson." His name was a household word from the Panhandle to the Gulf; from the Colorado to the Rio Grande, and the stories of his wit, prowess and adventures were sent abroad in the nation by press and pulpit. While the question of frontier protection was being considered in the United States Congress in 1872, a Texas member said in his speech: "Remove your regulars from the garrison on the Texas border; commission Jack Potter, a reclaimed desperado and now a Methodist preacher and Indian fighter, instruct him to choose and organize one hundred men and Indian depredations along the Texas border will cease."

Rev. I. G. John, a Methodist preacher, filled an appointment on York's Creek. Potter went out to hear him, more for the novelty of the meeting and a spirit of curiosity. The text, "Who is the wise man?" pierced his soul, and from that day he became a regular attendant at preaching, even denying himself the pleasures of a Sunday race in order to hear Rev. John preach.

John preached at a great religious revival held at Croft's Prairie, in 1856. Mr. Potter was converted, joined the church and the horse racer, gambler and saloonkeeper tough was completely transformed and he became one of the most useful men West Texas ever knew.

[Having served in the U.S. Army during the Mexican War and the Confederate Army during the Civil War,] in the fall of 1865 Mr. Potter was appointed as a supply to the Prairie Lea circuit and at the annual conference held at Seguin in the fall of 1867, he was sent to the mountain frontier and took station at Kerrville. This threw him in the region where, on each light moon, the Indian left his trail of blood along some mountainside or valley. But the Comanche yell had no terrors for Potter; he had heard it before and had been schooled in all their wiles and methods. In 1868 Mr. Potter bought a place near Boerne and moved his family to it. In 1871 he was sent to the Uvalde circuit, which bordered on the Rio Grande, where Indians could cross any day, and their depredations, killing and stealing, were almost of daily occurrence. Uvalde, at that time, was known as one of the wickedest places on the border and never before had preaching. In addition to his ministerial work, Mr. Potter had been appointed colporteur, and over this vast territory he distributed among rich and poor alike a great number of Bibles.

During the first year of his work in the mountain region the Indians made a raid on Curry's Creek. Dr. Nowlin, an old frontiersman, knew the Indians were in the country and stationed two men in his corncrib to guard his horses, which were loose in the lot. The moon was at its full and along about midnight two Indians were seen to stealthily approach, and as they began to let down the lot fence, one of the men in the crib took good aim and fired, killing the Indian in his tracks, the other man was so scared he could not shoot and the other Indian got away. While on his rounds in the Uvalde work, on the road between the Frio and Sabinal Canyon, Mr. Potter met a squad of four Indians. He was traveling in an ambulance drawn by two small Spanish mules and while passing through a lonely defile in the mountains he came up almost face to face with these four redskins. He saw there was going to be a fight and, seizing his Winchester, he leaped out of his ambulance and securely tied his mules to a sapling and then, under cover of a thicket, he reached a slight elevation, where he could better command a full view of the enemy. Getting in a good position, the parson took good aim and pulled the trigger, but the gun failed to fire and the "click" of the hammer revealed his whereabouts. Two Indians had citizen rifles and blazed away at him, but without effect. The parson fired at the same instant, wounding one of the Indians and knocking the gun out of his hands. The wounded Indian was taken up by his comrades and carried off.

Potter might have killed all four before they got out of reach, but he was afraid to risk his cartridges, as they had been on hand some time. Returning to his ambulance, he drove off some distance from the road and came to the foot of a mountain and drove into a dense thicket. He knew there were more than four Indians around, and that they were likely to lay in ambush somewhere ahead. When he had secured his team in the thicket he carefully cleaned his gun, selected the best cartridges, got his pistol in fighting trim, and began to look around. He discovered two Indians watching for him from the summit of the hill above him and when they saw that he had seen them, they blazed away, but missed their mark. Mr. Potter pumped several shots at them as they scampered over the hill out of sight. He then re-entered his vehicle and drove away without seeing that bunch of redskins again.

One instance out of many, will give the reader an idea of the person, the men and the times of which we write. While on this frontier work, late one evening he reached a military outpost. It might have been Fort Clark. The soldiers had just been paid off and the little village near the post was crowded with gamblers, sharpers, crooks and other disreputable characters. Many of these knew Mr. Potter and when he rode up they set up a shout, "Here comes the fighting parson!" "Hold up, there, old pardner! Can't you give us a gospel song an' dance tonight?" When told he would preach to them if they would provide a place, one sang out, "Sure, Parson, we'll make way for ye, if we have to rent the saloon!" A saloon gallery was provided with rude seats, kegs, barrels and a few chairs from dwellings nearby, and as the word had gone abroad that a strange preacher was in town, people began to assemble early. One man who was the worse for drink, insisted on acting the part of usher and town crier. He mounted a barrel and for some time kept up the cry, "O yes. O yes. O yes! There is going to be some hellfired racket here, right here on this gallery by fightin' Parson Potter, a reformed gambler, but now a regular gospel shark. The jig will begin now in fifteen minutes, and you old whiskey soaks and card sharpers, come over and learn how to mend your ways, or the devil will get you quicker'n hell can scorch a feather."

A great crowd assembled—one of the hardest looking sets of human beings Potter had ever preached to, but they kept good order, and when service concluded they wanted to "set'em up" to the parson, but when he declined that mark of their respect they passed an empty cigar box and all "chipped in." He preached the next day and was pressed by those rude Western men to come again and come often.

In 1878 or 1879 Mr. Potter began his labors at Fort Concho. San Angelo was a small frontier village and, like all post towns along the border, had a record not the best along the liens of morality. The saloons and gambling halls were popular resorts. They were open day and night, and every man went heavily armed. Mr. Potter visited the families, preached to the gamblers, soldiers and plainsmen.

As has been stated, no man who ever lived in Southwest Texas was more widely known than A. J. Potter. That he acquired the title of the "fighting parson" was in no wise derogatory to his character as a man, a Christian gentleman or a preacher. He was a man absolutely without fear. He was never the aggressor, and when a difficulty was forced upon him he always acted on the defensive and vanquished his assailant. His personal combats with Indians and desperadoes would fill a volume. It is a notable fact that when he had overcame an assailant in a fist fight or otherwise, if he chanced to be a white man, he always gave him fatherly counsel and offered him his hand.[1]

More on the Fighting Parson's Son

◆ Jack Potter (1920)

I will never forget seeing that train come into Dodge City that night. Old "Dog Face" and his bunch were pretty badly frightened and we had considerable difficulty in getting them aboard.

It was about 12:30 when the train pulled out. The conductor came around and I gave him my cowboy ticket. It was almost as long as your arm, and as he tore off a chunk of it I said: "What authority have you to tear up a man's ticket?" He laughed and said, "You are on my division. I simply tore off one coupon and each conductor between here and San Antonio will tear off one for each division." That sounded all right, but I wondered if that ticket would hold out all the way down.

Everyone seemed to be tired and worn out and the bunch began bedding down. Old Dog Face was out of humor, and was the last one to bed down. At about three o'clock our train was sidetracked to let the westbound train pass. This little stop caused the boys to sleep all the sounder. Just then the westbound train sped by traveling at the rate of about forty miles an hour, and just as it passed our coach the engineer blew the whistle.

Talk about your stampedes! That bunch of sleeping cowboys arose as one man, and started on the run with old Dog Face Smith in the lead. I was a little slow in getting off, but fell in with the drags. I had not yet woke up, but thinking I was in a genuine cattle stampede, yelled out, "Circle your leaders and keep up the drags." Just then the leaders circled and ran into the drags, knocking some of us down. They circled again and the news butcher crawled out from under foot and jumped through the window like a frog. Before they could circle back the next time, the train crew pushed in the door and caught old Dog Face and soon the bunch quieted down. The conductor was pretty angry and threatened to have us transferred to the freight department and loaded into a stock car.[1]

•• George W. Saunders (1920)

Jack Potter once told me that while he was up in this part of Kansas he got lost from his outfit one night and rode up to one of these dugouts and asked if he could stop with them until morning. The granger told him he was welcome to do so, although their accommodations were very limited.

They fed his horse for him and then invited him down into the dugout, which contained one room about sixteen feet square, but as neat as could be. In this room there was a nice clean bed, one table, four chairs, a stove, cooking utensils, the man, his wife and two small boys.

The wife soon prepared a good supper for Jack, and after he had eaten they sat up and talked to him for quite a while, during which time the little boys fell asleep on the bed, while the parents, who seemed to be a very intelligent couple, told Jack about themselves and their plans. They were enthusiastic over the prospects to make a fortune in that new country, and talked about everything in general, but all this time Jack was puzzling his brain over how all of them were going to sleep on the one bed in that dugout.

Finally the mother picked up the two boys and sat them over in a corner, leaning them against the wall still asleep, and then she informed Jack that he could occupy the bed and she and her husband went up the steps. Potter turned in and was soon asleep, and slept soundly all night long, but when he awoke the next morning he found himself sitting in the corner with the two little boys and the man and woman were occupying the bed. After breakfast he gave them five dollars, but they protested, saying that fifty cents was enough to pay for the poor accommodations he had received, but Jack informed them that what he had seen and learned right there was worth five dollars to him.[2]

Joel Collins

A question exists about whether Joel Collins was part of the Ware/ Lockridge trail drive from Austin to Nebraska City in 1871, as claimed by Charley Hester. Joseph, James, and Joel Collins had ranched around Goliad in Southeast Texas for several years immediately after the Civil War. The brothers' partnership broke up around 1871, with Joseph subsequently going on to become a prominent rancher.[1]

The Life and Adventures of Sam Bass states that Joel trailed one thousand cattle north in the summer of '71 for the "Bennett and 'Schoate'" outfit of North Texas.[2] Written by an anonymous author in the late 1870s, the original edition of this book was published in dime novel format and is of questionable accuracy.

Complicating the issue of the Collins connection to Charley Hester is the fact that in 1936, Sam Bass historian Wayne Gard published a book that touched upon Collins's trail-herding activities in the early 1870s. Unfortunately, on this particular aspect he copied the aforementioned anonymous Bass book virtually word for word, including a major error in the name of the outfit with which Collins was alleged to have ridden in 1871.[3]

Both the anonymous version of Collins's 1871 trail drive and the cloned Gard version have problems, since the Choate (not Schoate) ranch was headquartered near Helena in South Texas (not North Texas) and was *always* called the Choate and Bennett (not Bennett and Choate) by the men who rode for it (and also by Charley Hester—see chapter 22).[4]

The anonymous Sam Bass book was hastily written immediately after Bass's death at the hands of Texas Rangers with an apparent goal of cashing in on the widespread publicity surrounding that particular shootout. Given that the supposed name of Joel Collins's 1871 drive is wrong, it is not inconceivable that other details also are wrong— and perhaps manufactured in the haste to get the book to the public before interest waned. Furthermore, the authority the anonymous author used to put Joel Collins in the Choate and Bennett (as opposed to

Ware/Lockridge) operation is unknown and unstated. A writer making a guess at what organization a man trailed with in 1871 could do much worse than to arbitrarily pick the very prominent Choate and Bennett—an outfit that moved multiple herds in a single season—as opposed to a minor, unknown operation such as Ware/Lockridge.

It is also possible Ware/Lockridge was a subcontractor for the Choate and Bennett or the herd was on consignment from them; as a green eighteen-year-old, Charley Hester could have misunderstood its ownership makeup at the time, or his memory could have failed him over the seven decades between the trail drive and his telling of its story.

In any event, the record shows that Joel Collins and Charley Hester both rode the Chisholm Trail that year and both were in Abilene at the same time. Whether they came up the trail together is open to debate. The opinion one reaches on the matter depends largely upon whether one relies on a book written by an anonymous author whose sources are unknown and published in an effort to make a quick profit in the aftermath of a celebrated outlaw's widely publicized and bloody death.

§

The record is undisputed in regard to Joel Collins's later career—the one of outlawry referred to by Charley Hester. Collins moved herds up the trail the next few seasons following the '71 drive. After suffering losses in 1874 due to a downturn in the cattle market, Joel decided to change professions and in 1875 became a part owner in a San Antonio saloon.[5]

Within a few months Sam Bass appeared on the scene, and the two began a joint enterprise based upon gambling. Dealing monte and racing horses, Collins and Bass spent their time traveling between San Antonio and Mexico for the next year. Then, in April 1876, Collins sold his interest in the saloon, bought a herd on credit, and in partnership with Bass had it heading north by summertime. It appears from various reports that the cattle were sold in Kansas and that the money was then used to buy more cattle in Ogallala, which were then herded to Deadwood in the Dakota Territory.[6]

Here the two took the first steps into their journey on the wrong side of the law. Retaining the profits from the sale of the cattle in Deadwood, Collins and Bass began their new career by cheating their Texas financial backers out of their share of the proceeds.[7]

Collins used part of these funds to buy into a dance hall and house of ill repute in Deadwood. Interests were also purchased in a quartz mine and a freighting operation. As these business concerns began to fail, reports soon followed that Collins had swindled two local operations out of nine hundred head of cattle. At the same time Collins and Bass began to associate themselves with other men of dubious character.[8]

As the leader of a six-man gang, Collins began robbing stage-coaches around March 1877. The enterprise got off to an inauspicious start when one of the group intemperately opened fire during the first robbery, killing the driver.[9]

The outlaws nonetheless continued with their new occupation and committed six or seven more holdups. Competition in the field was brisk as other bandits sought to take their share of the bounties of the Black Hills, and before long the stage companies took steps to deter the thefts. Consequently, within a few short weeks the golden age of stagecoach robberies in the Black Hills had passed.[10]

Looking for easier targets, Collins decided to rob the Union Pacific Railroad, and the group proceeded to Ogallala to scout out opportunities. Venturing into western Nebraska in late August, the men had but six horses, a pack mule, and $40 in cash to their names.[11]

Within a short time they put a plan together, which was implemented on the night of September 18, 1877. Surprising the station agent at Big Springs, Nebraska, Collins had a red lantern placed to signal the eastbound train that passengers or mail were there for pick-up.[12]

Seeing the light, the unsuspecting engineer stopped as he was required to do and the outlaws quickly took control of the train. Entering the freight car, they were obliged to ignore 535 bars of silver stacked on the floor totaling over fifty thousand pounds in weight and $682,000 in value. Despite the great frustration the men must have felt in having to bypass this fortune, all was not lost as they came across a gold shipment of $60,000 in newly minted coin bound for Wells Fargo and the National Bank of Commerce in New York. Not content with the gold, the outlaws also relieved the passengers of their personal funds—a sum amounting to several hundred dollars more.[13]

In mounting their getaway the robbers quickly decided to split up. The massive manhunt that would be undertaken would focus on a group, and a couple of men would be less likely to draw the attention of a posse. After taking an oath around a campfire not to be taken alive, the members split off into three pairs, with Collins and Bill Potts (a.k.a. Bill Heffridge) heading straight south.[14]

Moving into Kansas, things were going uneventfully for the duo until they came upon the Kansas Pacific tracks at Buffalo Station (now Park). Unbeknownst to Collins and Potts, a squad of the 16th U.S. Infantry had arrived from Fort Hays to watch for the train robbers. Joining the soldiers was Ellis County sheriff George Bardsley.[15]

With Collins approaching them in the early morning hours, a strange drama unfolded, as Collins asked what was going on and received a response that the soldiers and sheriff were on the lookout for Joel Collins and his gang. Nonetheless, Collins lingered about the hamlet for over a half hour and actually gave his real name a couple of times when asked. At one point, while paying for supplies, Collins pulled papers out of his pocket, one of which had his name inscribed on it. The storekeeper asked him if his name was Joel Collins and Collins replied in the affirmative. The storekeeper immediately went to the sheriff and told him, but the sheriff discounted the notion that this stranger was the same Joel Collins that was being sought. Furthermore, the storekeeper later stated he also did not think this Joel Collins was the Joel Collins being hunted. To add to the course of events, a civilian who had met Collins before but who could not recall the particulars coincidentally happened to be at the outpost and exchanged pleasantries with him. Still no alarm was sounded. Amazingly, it did not occur to anyone in town that this was their man.[16]

Eventually Collins and Potts headed south at a leisurely pace. Undeterred by the soldiers, undeterred by the sheriff, undeterred by the contact with the acquaintance, and undeterred by the store clerk seeing his name on the paperwork, Collins exhibited a marked lack of concern in getting out of the area. As the fugitives were casually disappearing, one of the soldiers started questioning whether it might not be a good idea to at least detain the men.

Sheriff Bardsley decided to have another talk with the two drifters heading south. Riding after them he engaged them in a brief conversation, during which Collins once again confirmed his name to sheriff. The sheriff was still unconvinced and rode back to Buffalo Station and told the soldiers these were not the men being sought. [17]

Disgusted with the whole matter, an enlisted man decided enough was enough and went after the riders with some of the other soldiers. Sheriff Bardsley thereupon decided it would do no harm to at least hold the strangers until they could be checked out. As the group chased down Collins and Potts, the outlaws allowed themselves to be overtaken. Upon being told they were going to be detained, Collins and Potts pulled their weapons and exchanged gunfire with the posse. [18]

When the smoke cleared, both outlaws were dead. True to their oath to the rest of the train robbers, they were not taken alive. Over $20,000 in gold was found on their horses. [19]

After Collins's demise Sam Bass formed his own, more renowned gang, which was as short-lived as the first group. Ten months after Collins and Potts were shot to death in Kansas, Sam Bass met his own fate in a hail of bullets from Texas Rangers at Round Rock, Texas. [20]

Charley's Acquaintance with E. S. Sutton

➥ Charley Hester (ca. 1939)

I've been a talkin' about myself, but now Everette I will tell you about my introduction to the Suttons and yourself. Of Course you won't remember it, but what matter, I do.

As I drove to town I often met your father and mother as they walked from the Naponee depot to the river. A fine looking couple they were, and friendly like. Between them was swung a basket and in the basket a baby.

One evening I decided to pull up and talk a bit. But when they stopped, a regular hurricane of flying hands and feet broke loose in the basket, and of all the squawking I ever heard, it beat the bobcats in the thickets—My, oh my, what a lot of noise from such a little thing!

Your father smiled serenely, nodded his head toward you and said: "He is hungry. He thinks he is a through freight and won't stand for a delay." And your mother proudly contributed her bit: "Yes. And we are going to the river for lunch."

Well! Well! Thought I, a paddle where a paddle belongs would be my remedy for that spoiled brat.

Arriving home I heard a somewhat similar bedlam and my wife sings out: "Charley, baby's hungry, maybe needs a change—walk him while I set up the food." And I walked him, bless his heart. It all depends on whose baby is bawling whether it's noise or whether it's music.[1]

➥ Kirby Ross (2003)

Everette S. Sutton Jr., whose crying irritated Charley so much, was born in Naponee a year after the Hester family arrived in the region. Everette's father was the Burlington Railroad's local agent, thus Charley's references to the Naponee depot and the metaphorical "through freight." The Sutton family moved from Naponee to Colorado in 1895, but two decades later fate brought Charley and Everette

Jr. back together, this time in Dundy County. There Sutton, following in his father's footsteps, spent fifty-eight years working in Max and Benkelman as an agent for the Burlington Railroad.[2]

Sutton also engaged "in the study of the history of the west and [came] to be regarded as an authority in several fields of historical research."[3] Engaging in conversations with old-timers over the years and "being an early-day historian," Sutton would "record these stories, unknown to the yarn-teller, and [file] them away."[4]

In addition to the half-century acquaintance between Charley and Everette, Sutton's future wife, Hazel, and Charley's daughter Orpha (born 1903) were together at the Parks school from 1913 through 1915—Hazel as teacher and Orpha as student. Charley was running the Riverside Ranch two miles away at the time.[5]

Notes

Geography of Two Trails Traveled

1. Probably Sam P. Ridings, *The Chisholm Trail* (Guthrie OK: Cooperative Publishing, 1936).

2. For more on E. S. Sutton see the introduction and "Charley's Acquaintance with E. S. Sutton," this volume.

"Southdown Country"

1. For statistics on the livestock in the county, see Francis A. Walker, *The Statistics of the Wealth and Industry of the United States, Ninth Census* (Washington DC: Government Printing Office, 1872), 250–61; *Report on the Productions of Agriculture as Returned at the Tenth Census* (Washington DC: Government Printing Office, 1883), 170–72. See also George W. Tyler, *The History of Bell County* (San Antonio TX: Naylor, 1936).

The Abilene Cattle Market Crash

1. Joseph G. McCoy, *Historic Sketches of the Cattle Trade* (Kansas City MO: Ramsey, Millett & Hudson, 1874), 226–28.

Ware/Lockridge

1. For legal documentation regarding Charley's boss's use of an alias, see *Hubbell Johnson against a certain person or persons the owner or owners of a drove of cattle known as Cherokee cattle now being driven through Jefferson County Nebraska by said owner or owners of said cattle known as Lockridge and by some as Ware*, Papers of 1871, Box A, Jefferson County (NE) Probate Court, October 11, 1871.

2. See the *Caldwell (KS) Journal*, September 20, 1883, and December 20, 1883 (both reports reprinted from the Darlington, Indian Territory, *Cheyenne Transporter*).

The Prairie Fire

1. See Denise Gess and William Lutz, *Firestorm at Peshtigo: A Town, Its People, and the Deadliest Fire in American History* (New York: Henry Holt, 2002).

2. For the legal proceedings related to the fire, see *Hubble Johnson & John*

Doe, Day Book 1866–1871, p. 335, Jefferson County (NE) Probate Court, October 11, 1871; *Hubbell Johnson against a certain person*.

John Wesley Hardin

1. For more regarding the anonymity under which Hardin operated while in Abilene, see *The Prairie Scout*, vol. 2 (Abilene TX: Kansas Corral of the Westerners, 1974), 1–29.

2. John Wesley Hardin, *The Life of John Wesley Hardin* (Seguin TX: Smith & Moore, 1896), 5–60; Richard C. Marohn, *The Last Gunfighter: John Wesley Hardin* (College Station TX: Creative Publishing, 1995), 11–43. At page 41, Marohn offers an objective pro and con presentation of the evidence relating to the snoring legend and in the process tilts the debate against such an event having occurred.

The Death of Hickok

1. For the shooting of Coe in Abilene and the legends that surrounded Mc-Call's murder of Hickok in Deadwood, see Joseph G. Rosas, *Wild Bill Hickok: The Man and His Myth* (Lawrence: University of Kansas Press, 1996). For a thoroughly researched account of the death of Hickok and McCall's statements about it, see Thadd Turner, *Wild Bill Hickok: Deadwood City—End of Trail* (Deadwood SD: Out West Alive Publishing, 2001).

The Ranches of '78

1. *History of the State of Nebraska* (Chicago: Western Historical Company, 1882), 1389; *Compendium of History Reminiscence and Biography of Western Nebraska* (Chicago: Alden Publishing, 1909), 347–48; Marianne Brinda Beel, ed., *A Sandhill Century: The People* (Valentine NE: Cherry County Centennial Committee, 1985), 240.

2. *History of the State of Nebraska*, 651–52, 1385, 1389; *Compendium*, 348; *A Sandhill Century: The People*, 240.

3. *A Sandhill Century: The People*, 240; Marianne Brinda Beel, ed., *A Sandhill Century: The Land* (Valentine NE: Cherry County Centennial Committee, 1986), 37; Charles S. Reece, *A History of Cherry County, Nebraska* (Simeon NE, 1945) 17, 19.

4. *A Sandhill Century: The People*, 240.

5. *Railroad and County Map of Nebraska* (Chicago: Geo. F. Cram Engraver and Publisher, 1883).

6. *History of the State of Nebraska*, 1385; *A Sandhill Century: The People*, 240; *A Sandhill Century: The Land*, 37; *A History of Cherry County*, 90–91; *Compendium*, 348.

7. *A Sandhill Century: The People*, 240.

8. *Compendium*, 348.

9. *Compendium*, 347; *A Sandhill Century: The People*, 240–41.

10. J. Marvin Hunter, ed., *The Trail Drivers of Texas*, vol. 1 (San Antonio TX: Jackson Printing, 1920), 190.

11. *Frio County, Texas: A History* (Pearsall TX: Frio Pioneer Jail Museum Association, 1979), 130; Collis Roy Woodward Sr., family research, forwarded to Kirby Ross by Carol Woodward Noble; John Oge Flannery Jr., "Ancestors of Louis Adolphe Oge," Oge Genealogy and Fact Sheet, October 7, 2001. Collis Roy Woodward and Carol Noble are father and daughter, and are the grandson and great-granddaughter of Montcalen Woodward. John Oge Flannery Jr. is the great-grandson of Louis Oge.

12. Flannery, "Ancestors"; *Frio County, Texas*, 102–3; Wayne R. Austerman, *Sharps Rifles and Spanish Mules* (College Station: Texas A&M Press, 1985), 28, 56, 316. Legends have arisen that Oge was an orphan when he went to work on the John Woodward ranch in 1847 at age fifteen. However, church and census records indicate his father, Adolphe, was alive at least until 1850. See Flannery, "Ancestors."

13. *Frio County, Texas*, 102–3; Flannery, "Ancestors".

14. *Frio County, Texas*, 103, 130, 132; Jemmie Newton Clark, *Pioneer Newtons of Southwest Texas* (Redlands CA, 1959), 84–85; Collis Woodward Sr., family research.

15. *Frio County, Texas*, 132–33; Louis B. James, "Woodward, First Century on the Sand-Sage Prairie, 1887–1987," *Chronicles of Oklahoma* 64 (Fall 1986).

16. Flannery, "Ancestors"; Clark, *Pioneer Newtons*, 57; *Frio County, Texas*, 103, 130; J. L. Hiler, "History of Frio County," 4–5 (unpublished, undated typescript written ca. 1940s, in the possession of James H. Hiler, Pearsall TX); Mrs. W. A. Roberts, "Frio County Has a Colorful History," *Frontier Times*,

June 1936, 453–59; J. Marvin Hunter, ed., *The Trail Drivers of Texas*, vol. 2 (San Antonio TX: Jackson Printing, 1923), 119; Hunter, *The Trail Drivers of Texas*, vol. 1, 233.

17. Flannery, "Ancestors"; *Frio County, Texas*, 103, 130–31; "City of San Antonio Officers: 1837–1983" (list compiled by the San Antonio Public Library, Texana/Genealogy Department).

18. Flannery, "Ancestors"; *Frio County, Texas*, 103, 130–31, 133; Mont Woodward obituary, December 14, 1904, *Arizona Republican*; Collis Woodward Sr., family research.

Javeline Hogs and Rattlesnakes

1. *Frio County, Texas*, 84; Annie Tom (Hiler) Tillotson, "Hiler Family" (typescript in the possession of James H. Hiler of Pearsall TX); James H. Hiler, family group record sheets and miscellaneous genealogical data compiled from various family sources; Alice Hiler Wager-Smith, "Pillow Slips Made and Data Researched 1931–1977" (manuscript distributed within Hiler family outlining various nineteenth- and twentieth-century brands used by the family, as well as copies of old family correspondence with historical data); Anita (Hiler) Cahoon, correspondence to Kirby Ross, July 11, 2001; James H. Hiler, correspondence and map to Kirby Ross, January 22, 2001, June 6, 2002, July 27, 2002, and November 2, 2002.

2. *Frio County, Texas*; Tillotson, "Hiler Family"; James H. Hiler, family group records; Anita (Hiler) Cahoon, correspondence; Florence Fenley, *Oldtimers: Their Own Stories* (Uvalde TX: Hornby Press, 1939), 31.

3. J. L. Hiler, "History of Frio County," 4–5.

4. Roberts, "Frio County Has a Colorful History"; *Frio County, Texas*.

5. Fenley, *Oldtimers*, 31.

6. *Frio County, Texas*; Tillotson, "Hiler Family."

7. *Frio County, Texas*; Tillotson, "Hiler Family."

8. *Frio County, Texas*; Tillotson, "Hiler Family"; Roberts, "Frio County Has a Colorful History."

9. Wager-Smith; Tillotson, "Hiler Family"; James H. Hiler, family group records; Mrs. Lee Hiler, "Lee Reavis Hiler," (unpublished, undated typescript in the possession of James H. Hiler).

10. James H. Hiler, family group records; Anita (Hiler) Cahoon, correspondence; Tillotson, "Hiler Family".

Huffmeyer's Experience

1. Born in 1856, Adolph Huffmeyer was the son of Katherine Oge Huffmeyer, sister of Louis Oge. Flannery, "Ancestors of Louis Adolphe Oge."

2. Virgil A. Johnson (1842–1914) was the brother-in-law of Caven Woodward and Louis Oge. Jemmie Newton Clark, *Pioneer Newtons of Southwest Texas*, 84–85.

3. One of which appears to have been the Lee herd, in which Charley Hester was a top-hand.

4. Hunter, ed., *The Trail Drivers of Texas*, vol. 1, 233–39.

Custer and Hester

1. See the historical markers at Republican Forks and Roundhole on U.S. 34 and K-161 between Benkelman, Nebraska, and Bird City, Kansas. See also General G. A. Custer, *My Life on the Plains* (New York, 1876), 54–78, and Minnie Dubbs Milbrook, "The West Breaks in General Custer," *Kansas Historical Quarterly* 36 (Summer 1970): 113–48.

The Dull Knife Raid

1. George Bird Grinnell, *The Fighting Cheyennes* (New York: Charles Scribner's Sons, 1915); Mari Sandoz, *Cheyenne Autumn* (New York: McGraw Hill, 1953).

2. Grinnell, *The Fighting Cheyennes*; Sandoz, *Cheyenne Autumn*; William Y. Chalfant, *Cheyennes at Dark Water Creek* (Norman: University of Oklahoma Press, 1997); John H. Monnett, *Massacre at Cheyenne Hole* (Niwot: University Press of Colorado, 1999); Evelyn M. Ward, "The Battle between Buffalo Hunters and Indians," *Sherman County Historical Newsletter* 34:4 (April 2002).

3. Grinnell, *The Fighting Cheyennes*; Sandoz, *Cheyenne Autumn*; *Decatur County Then and Now* (Oberlin KS: Oberlin Diamond Jubilee Book Committee, 1960), 3–5.

4. Grinnell, *The Fighting Cheyennes*; Sandoz, *Cheyenne Autumn*; *Decatur County Then and Now*. In the 1950s Charley Hester's biographer E. S. Sutton corresponded fairly extensively with Mari Sandoz, including about aspects of

Cheyenne Alumn. See Sandoz Research Files, Box 30, Mari Sandoz Collection, Archives and Special Collections, University of Nebraska–Lincoln Libraries; Sandoz Correspondence Files, Boxes 21, 22, 23, 24, 28, 31, 36, Mari Sandoz Collection,Archives and Special Collections, University of Nebraska–Lincoln Libraries.

The Grand Central Hotel Fire

1. James W. Savage and John T. Bell, *History of the City of Omaha Nebraska* (New York: Munsell, 1894), 253–54.

The Killing of Ketchum and Mitchell

1. *History of the State of Nebraska*, 331, 542–44; S. D. Butcher, *Pioneer History of Custer County, and Short Sketches of Early Days in Nebraska* (n.p.: Broken Bow, 1901), 43–62.

2. *History of the State of Nebraska*, 331, 542–44; Butcher, *Pioneer History of Custer County*, 43–62; I. P. Olive and Frederick Fisher v. The State of Nebraska, 9 Neb. 3 (1881).

3. *Denver Tribune-Republican*, August 18, 1886, 1; Harry E. Chrisman, *Lost Trails of the Cimarron* (Denver: Sage Books, 1961), 107–8, 225.

The Fighting Parson

1. Hunter, ed., *The Trail Drivers of Texas*, vol. 1, 250.

More on the Fighting Parson's Son

1. Hunter, ed., *The Trail Drivers of Texas*, vol. 1, 55.
2. Hunter, ed., *The Trail Drivers of Texas*, vol. 1, 394.

Joel Collins

1. Paula Reed and Grover Ted Tate, *The Tenderfoot Bandits: Sam Bass and Joel Collins, Their Lives and Hard Times* (Tucson AZ: Westernlore Press, 1988), 34; Rick Miller, *Sam Bass and Gang* (Austin TX: State House Press, 1999), 35.

2. Anonymous, *Life and Adventures of Sam Bass: The Notorious Union Pacific and Texas Train Robber* (Dallas: Dallas Commercial Steam Print, 1878), 18.

3. Anonymous, *Life and Adventures of Sam Bass*; Wayne Gard, *Sam Bass* (Boston: Houghton Mifflin, 1936), 51.

4. Hunter, ed., *The Trail Drivers of Texas*, vol. 1 (San Antonio TX: Jackson Printing, 1920), 21, 102–3, 230–31, 266, 389, 392, 394, 414, 468.

5. Reed and Tate, *Tenderfoot Bandits*, 33; Miller, *Sam Bass and Gang*, 36.

6. Reed and Tate, *Tenderfoot Bandits*, 34–37, 89; Miller, *Sam Bass and Gang*, 36, 39–46.

7. Miller, *Sam Bass and Gang*, 46.

8. Reed and Tate, *Tenderfoot Bandits*, 90; Miller, *Sam Bass and Gang*, 47–48.

9. Reed and Tate, *Tenderfoot Bandits*, 94; Miller, *Sam Bass and Gang*, 51–52.

10. Reed and Tate, *Tenderfoot Bandits*, 96–97; Miller, *Sam Bass and Gang*, 55–62.

11. Miller, *Sam Bass and Gang*, 63.

12. Reed and Tate, *Tenderfoot Bandits*, 97–98; Miller, *Sam Bass and Gang*, 64.

13. Reed and Tate, *Tenderfoot Bandits*, 100; Miller, *Sam Bass and Gang*, 65–70.

14. Reed and Tate, *Tenderfoot Bandits*, 102; Miller, *Sam Bass and Gang*, 80.

15. Reed and Tate, *Tenderfoot Bandits*, 103; Miller, *Sam Bass and Gang*, 81–82, 85.

16. Reed and Tate, *Tenderfoot Bandits*, 103–5; Miller, *Sam Bass and Gang*, 85–88.

17. Reed and Tate, *Tenderfoot Bandits*, 104–5; Miller, *Sam Bass and Gang*, 89–90.

18. Reed and Tate, *Tenderfoot Bandits*, 104–5; Miller, *Sam Bass and Gang*, 89–90.

19. Reed and Tate, *Tenderfoot Bandits*, 105; Miller, *Sam Bass and Gang*, 90.

20. Reed and Tate, *Tenderfoot Bandits*, 193–239; Miller, *Sam Bass and Gang*, 234–62.

Charley's Acquaintance with E. S. Sutton

1. From the Hester memoir.

2. U.S. Bureau of the Census, *Thirteenth U.S. Census, Barr Precinct No. 5, Adams County, Colorado* (1910); U.S. Bureau of the Census, *Fourteenth U.S. Census, Max Township, Dundy County, Nebraska* (1920); *Benkelman Post*, May 6, 1987, 7.

3. *Benkelman Post*, January 4, 1968, 1.

4. *McCook (NE) Daily Gazette*, May 11, 1968, 4.

5. Faris, ed., *Who's Who in Nebraska* (Lincoln: Nebraska Press Association, 1940), 411. Hazel married Everette in 1916.